Censored Screams

729-1

Censored Screams

The British Ban on Hollywood Horror in the Thirties

TOM JOHNSON

with forewords by
Richard Gordon *and*
Tom Weaver

afterword by
Greg Mank

McFarland & Company, Inc., Publishers
Jefferson, North Carolina, and London

Frontispiece: Creator (Colin Clive) and Monster (Boris Karloff) take a break in *Bride of Frankenstein* (1935).

British Library Cataloguing-in-Publication data are available

Library of Congress Cataloguing-in-Publication Data

Johnson, Tom, 1947–
    Censored screams : the British ban on Hollywood horror in the
thirties / Tom Johnson ; with forewords by Richard Gordon and Tom
Weaver. Afterword by Greg Mank.
      p.   cm.
    Filmography: p.
    Includes bibliographical references and index.
    ISBN 0-7864-0394-2 (library binding : 50# alkaline paper) ∞
    1. Horror films—History and criticism.   2. Motion pictures—
Censorship—Great Britain.   I. Title.
PN1995.9.H6J65   1997
791.43'6164—dc21   97-14733
                                             CIP

Manufactured in the United States of America

McFarland & Company, Inc., Publishers
  Box 611, Jefferson, North Carolina 28640

Table of Contents

Acknowledgments

My plan to research these events had its beginning in a conversation with Tom Weaver who, as usual, provided a stumbling author with more help than can be documented. He, along with Richard Gordon and Greg Mank, needs no introduction, but, just in case...

Tom is the author of a series of interview books (including *Interviews with B Science Fiction and Horror Movie Makers,* with John and Michael Brunas), *Poverty Row HORRORS!*, *Universal Horrors* (also with John and Michael Brunas), and countless articles in *Fangoria* and other magazines.

Richard Gordon has been involved with horror movies for over sixty years, first as a fan (which he steadfastly remains), then as a producer—certainly the only one to work with all of the Big Four: Boris Karloff, Bela Lugosi, Peter Cushing, and Christopher Lee. He is best known for *The Haunted Strangler* and *Corridors of Blood* (both with Karloff), *Fiend Without a Face,* and for the friendship and support he gives to fans and writers.

Greg Mank first burst on the scene with *It's Alive!* (the best Frankenstein book since Mary Shelley's), and followed it with, among others, *Karloff and Lugosi* and *Hollywood Cauldron,* in addition to many magazine contributions including *Films in Review.*

This trio's combined knowledge of horror movies would shame a computer, and I'm both pleased and grateful for their help.

Sincere thanks also to: Sue and Colin Cowie (who provided food and shelter in England and a wonderful illustration), the late Mike Royko and Mary Beth Pacer (*The Chicago Tribune*), Louis Paul (and the Lincoln Center for Performing Arts), the British Board of Film Classification, and the British Film Institute, Carol and Steve Werner, Elaine viii *Acknowledgments*

Hahn, Mark Miller, Randy Vest, and Becky and Brent Worley, who all answered various pleas for help, and Mike and John Brunas who supplied all stills not credited.

Following the destruction of the British Board of Film Censorship's office during World War II, most of the specific records relating to these incidents are gone; this book would have been impossible to write if not for the meticulous reporting of *The Kinematograph Weekly* and *Today's Cinema*.

Tom Johnson
Summer 1997

Foreword

by Tom Weaver

Censorship, like charity, should begin at home; but, unlike charity, it should end there.

—Clare Boothe Luce

You have a right to burn books or destroy books if you can prove they can do harm.

—Prof. Thomas Devine

The book you now hold deals with the British ban on horror films, the Hays Code and other related goings-on in the 1930s. Censorship and films, however, have gone together from the dawning days of the medium; in the nickelodeon era, the *Chicago Tribune* labeled them intolerably vicious, and an Illinois judge claimed that movies were responsible for "more juvenile crime coming into my court than all other causes combined." (The Chicago police department then previewed and licensed all films.) Censorship was an old story by the 1930s, when the horror genre was in its prime and British bluenoses who monitored such things got into such a snit they couldn't keep their teacups steady in their saucers.

Throughout the early years of "horror movie scholarship," England's ban on horror flicks was routinely credited with the 1936 demise of the genre. I never quite understood why Hollywood gave two hoots in a barn what censors on an island roughly the size of Ohio, half a world away, thought of horror films; there just *had* to be more to it than that. England, schmengland—sure enough, more recent research has shown that censors and concerned citizens in other countries (including our own) were up on their high horses, too. Also, and perhaps most importantly, horror films weren't registering at the box office like they had just a few short years before. The handwriting was on the wall, and Boris and Bela were soon ducking each other in the unemployment office. (That's the way *I* like to picture them, anyway.)

It's easy for smart-alecks to find fault with the censors, civic groups, angry parents, etc., who militated against the production of horror movies (*and* gangster movies, *and* ...) in the 1930s. But there are those who say that what the *anti*-censorship brigade has given us is our ugly modern entertainment world, in which a tub of vomit like *Hustler*'s Larry Flynt is celebrated as a First Amendment champion of folk hero status. "Parents should monitor what their kids watch and listen to!" shouts the anything-goes crowd, who feel like Big Brother is closing in if somebody suggests that maybe it isn't a good idea for violent or sexually explicit material to be shown on TV before the ungodly hour of, say, nine or ten at night. They think that the parents of today's kids should be available to watch TV with them at all times, listen to the radio with them at all times, supervise as they surf the Internet, keep a tight rein on them in bookstores and other places with dirty magazines at kid's eye level, etc., etc. What they're saying in effect is, *If you want to be a parent, never leave your kid's side, because I like violence/pornography to be easily accessible, and that's more important than your kid having anything resembling an innocent, old-fashioned childhood.* It seems to me that whenever one of these jokers is asked if he/she has children, the answer is always no. Thank God. (Too bad *their* parents didn't have that attitude!) Steve Allen recently called today's movie/TV industry "vulgarians entertaining barbarians," which has the ring to truth as far as I'm concerned. The FCC recently ruled that Howard Stern, who brought the cremated remains of one of his groupies onto his radio/TV show to rattle and play with them, did not exceed the bounds of decency in doing so. A tabloid newspaper paid a woman to lure Frank Gifford into a hotel room and secretly videotape their activities, and there are those who say his right to privacy has not been violated. It's scary to contemplate where we go from here. Should there be limits? I'll vote yes.

Now that I've identified myself as a prude, let's get back (finally!) to the horror movies of the 1930s. To me, part of the appeal of these movies is that they leave a lot to the imagination. By the late 1950s/early 1960s, this style of horror movie making was beginning to go the way of the dodo, and by the 1970s you had to have a cast-iron stomach to watch the average horror movie. I'll bet that a majority of the people reading this book have more fondness for the old-style horror films than the new ones; most horror fans of my acquaintance have zero interest in the ongoing antics of Jason, Freddy, Michael Myers, Pinhead, etc. I sometimes wonder how much sooner this "new era" of horror movies would have been upon us if not for "the purity patrol" (the Hays Office). If that sounds farout, remember that in the pre–Code *Murders in the Rue Morgue* Bela Lugosi wanted to find the Right Girl for his pet gorilla to have sex with. A man with sewn-shut lips gets a big screen–filling closeup in *Murders in the Zoo*. There's more proposed inter-species sex (and Charles Laughton being hacked to pieces by animal-men with surgical knives) in *Island of Lost Souls*. Those are just a few examples.

There was every indication that Hollywood intended to continue to "push the envelope": Before the Hays Office started flexing its muscles, the script of *The Black Cat* called for Bela Lugosi to put Boris Karloff on a rack, a prelude to the audience seeing in shadow "[Lugosi] splitting the scalp slowly, pulling the sheath of skin over [Karloff's] head and shoulders." We were then to see Karloff (sans skin) free himself, fall to the floor and, "still living as a hideous pulp of blood," drag his putrid body across the room toward the heroine. John L. Balderston sounded envious when he wrote in a memo to Universal that Cecil B. DeMille had "a monopoly on the great box office values of torture and cruelty"; he wanted to include in his script of *Dracula's Daughter* such scenes as a baby in a sack being presented to one of Dracula's ravenous vampire brides. If there were no censor's office to nix scenes like this, what would horror films have been like by the forties and fifties? If increasingly graphic movies were permissible and popular, would there have been no Val Lewton and movies like *Cat People*, more Dwain Espers and movies like *Maniac**? I don't know about you, but I like *The Lodger* and *The Wolf Man* without closeups of mangled victims; I like the fact that *The Ghost of Frankenstein* and *The Monster and the Girl* don't feature scenes in which the mad doctor is covered in blood, toting disembodied hands, feet and eyeballs around his lab. The modern horror crowd (not to mention our high-class friends the Hammerheads) may disagree with me, but I like these movies the way they are, and I'm grateful that what's happened to horror movies in the last 30 or 40 years was prevented from getting a good running headstart back in the mid-thirties.

*Esper's 1934 film features female nudity, a rape and a scene in which a mad scientist plucks out the eyeball of a cat and pops it into his mouth.

My opinion of the overall impact the censors happened to have on the old horror movies: To put words into the mouth of Boris Karloff's Monster, "Censor...*gooood*!" Read Tom Johnson's book and decide. And if you end up disagreeing with me, I don't want you goin' around *talking* about it, understand?

Foreword
by Richard Gordon

Tom Johnson has done a remarkable job of chronicling the history of horror film censorship in Great Britain. In doing so he revived many of my childhood memories about how my brother Alex and I clashed with the peculiarities of the system. (Alex Gordon has written and produced movies since the early fifties, including *The Day the World Ended, Voodoo Woman,* and *Requiem for a Gunfighter.* He's also a noted film historian and archivist and has been associated with Gene Autry for 40 years.)

In the early 1930s, we were oblivious to the problems as our filmgoing was limited to going with our parents. We usually saw a double feature program at least once a week. This changed when Alex was thirteen and I was ten and we were allowed to go out on our own. It then became a challenge to circumvent the regulations of the British Board of Film Censors and the London County Council.

The immediate problem was the "A" certificate that required a parent or guardian to accompany anyone under sixteen. There were two possibilities. One was to approach the box office, claim to be sixteen or over, and hope the cashier would not ask for proof of age. The second was to approach a sympathetic-looking single adult and ask to be taken in. This usually worked although occasionally there was a refusal, accompanied by a lecture on the immorality of trying to break the law.

Once in a while, a cinema manager would allow us in alone to an "A" program on condition that we sat next to an adult in case an inspector came around to check the audience. We thought of it as a friendly gesture but, in retrospect, it was probably more the desire to increase the box-office take as this generally happened at small out-of-the-way cinemas playing B movies and revivals.

Films rated "Adults Only" or with an "H" certificate were an insurmountable problem. I remember the ignominy of being turned away from a revival of the Boris Karloff film *The Ghoul*, despite being accompanied by our grandmother who valiantly tried to convince the manager that we were over sixteen. At least he had the decency not to suggest that she send us elsewhere and see the film on her own.

When Universal re-released *Frankenstein* and *Dracula* as a double bill in 1939, the program opened at the Rialto Theatre in London's West End and was a smash hit. Alex was then sixteen and I was thirteen but our parents agreed to see if we could all get in. I was refused admission. On this occasion, good manners dictated that I volunteer to see a "U" certificate film at another cinema, allowing them to enjoy the program. However, when the double bill went out on general re-release shortly thereafter, a schoolmate and I were able to see it at a suburban cinema where an usherette, who was a friend of my mate's mother, sneaked us in through the fire exit.

Son of Frankenstein arrived in London but by that time, I was taking no chances. I forged a school document to show that I was sixteen and got in to see it on my own.

While serving in the Royal Navy in World War II, I encountered a different kind of censorship. I was on active duty on a destroyer on which the chief medical officer was also in charge of security and censored all the mail. Alex was by then in the army and we liked to send each other detailed descriptions of the films we were able to see including the names of the cinemas and the dates. I found myself summoned to the CMO's cabin where I was told in no uncertain terms that my correspondence endangered the ship's security because if my letters were intercepted, the enemy could plot the ship's course and its movements by the information they contained, establishing a pattern. He didn't mind the synopses although he would have preferred them shorter!

My first professional experience with the BBFC occurred in 1946 when I had agreed to represent Excelsior Pictures of New York to try and sell their films in England. After I successfully licensed their film *The White Gorilla*, there arrived a screening print of an obscure older jungle melodrama called *Found Alive on the Delta of the Rio Grande*. It included scenes of the actual killing of snakes and other animals, to which the censors objected, and was banned in its entirety. Then Excelsior Pictures took on the distribution of *Freaks* on behalf of Dwain Esper and asked me to try and get it passed in England. It had been banned there since its original production in 1932.

I arranged an appointment at the offices of the BBFC where I was received quite civilly by an elderly lady who, from memory, resembled Dame May Whitty in *The Lady Vanishes*. However, when I started my business, the conversation came to an abrupt end. She stood up, went to the door, held it open for me and said "Mr. Gordon, we have nothing to discuss." The film was not permitted in Great Britain until the 1960s when it was finally approved with an "X" certificate that was requested by Antony Balch, a distributor who later became a film director and directed my two productions, *Secrets of Sex* and *Horror Hospital*.

Tom Johnson has wisely restricted this book to the horror genre. The peculiarities of the system, however, extended to many other categories. They could easily fill a second volume. For instance, there was the much-publicized battle between Walt Disney and the censors when they wanted to release *Snow White and the Seven Dwarfs* with an "A" certificate. Cecil B. DeMille's silent masterpiece *The King of Kings* was totally banned because the depiction of Jesus Christ on the screen was prohibited. *The Seashell and the Clergyman*, a famous French surrealist film, was banned because, although the viewing committee could not understand it, they were satisfied that had they been able to do so, they would have found its meaning objectionable.

Foreign language and art films as a whole were regarded differently than Hollywood and British pictures. The only film that ever frightened me out of my wits when I saw it as a child was Fritz Lang's German horror film, *The Testament of Dr. Mabuse*, which was shown with English subtitles and the Board therefore reckoned that it would play only in very few specialized cinemas.

There were special problems caused by so-called sex education films, and those that masqueraded as such, like *Damaged Lives*. They were allowed to be shown to adults only but there was a restriction on the type of film with which they could be double-billed. Nothing that smacked of exploitation was acceptable, resulting in the ludicrous situation that most cinemas simply put in a "U" certificate western to complete the program and most of the audience walked out before the western came on.

A friendly manager once allowed me to come in and see a Hoot Gibson western on condition that I left before the sex education film started. He made sure of it by personally escorting me back into the street.

Younger readers today may marvel about so much ado about nothing although, allowing for today's permissiveness, it hasn't changed all that much. The censors in Great Britain continue merrily on their idio-syncratic way, and America's MPAA rating system, under the influence of Jack Valenti, runs it a close second.

Richard Gordon, *October 1996*

Introduction

To be effective, horror movies—along with rock 'n' roll and skydiving—must be on the edge. In horror films, this edge separates good taste from bad, the acceptable from the unacceptable. The exact position of this line is elusive, and has shifted considerably since the thirties when the genre began. It has always, however, moved forward; each generation has required "more" to be horrified. Few things are less exciting than yesterday's frissons, as illustrated by Mike Royko's reflection in *The Chicago Tribune* (February 28, 1995), "Film Horrors of the Past Rate only a 'G' and a Yawn Today" (reprinted by permission: Tribune Media Services)—

> While walking through the video store, the 7 year-old boy stopped and gawked at a display of tapes. "Wow," he said, "what are those?"
>
> His father said, "Never mind. You don't want to watch those movies. They'll scare you, give you nightmares."
>
> The boy began reading the titles of the video boxes aloud. "*The Wolf Man*. Wow. *Frankenstein*. *Dracula*. Wow. *Frankenstein Meets the Wolf Man*. *The Mummy's Tomb*. Wow. What's a mummy?"
>
> The father explained, "A mummy is a very scary guy. They are all very scary."
>
> "Did you ever see them?" the boy asked.
>
> "Yes, all of them, a long time ago when I was a kid."
>
> "Did they scare you?"
>
> "I was so scared that I crawled under the seat in the movie theater and hid. People in the audience screamed and fainted."

1

"Cool, let's rent one."

"I told you. They are just too scary. You won't be able to sleep. And you might be the only kid in your class with gray hair."

"C'mon, please. Pleeeese."

They discussed it for a while, as modern families do, and finally negotiated a deal. The boy agreed that if he became too terrified, and closing his eyes and putting his head under a sofa cushion didn't protect his psyche, the father could switch the film off.

They walked out with three tapes—*Dracula*, for Friday night, *Frankenstein*, for Saturday night, and *Frankenstein Meets the Wolf Man*, for Sunday night.

"Can't we get that mummy movie too?" the boy asked.

"Your mother will kill me as it is," the father said.

He wasn't far off. "Are you crazy?" she said. "Those three movies over the weekend? By the time he gets back to school Monday, he'll be afraid to go to the bathroom alone."

"Don't worry. If it's too much for him, I'll hit the zapper."

"Why are you doing this?" she asked. "It's sadistic."

"No, it was his idea. Maybe he'll learn a lesson, that you should be careful about what you ask for."

That night they watched *Dracula*.

When the ship carrying the vampire's coffin arrived in England, and all the crew members were mysteriously dead, the boy asked: "What killed them?"

"Count Dracula. He got their blood."

"Why didn't we see that?"

"They didn't show stuff like that."

"Oh."

Later, a leering Dracula leaned slowly toward a sleeping woman's throat. But the scene ended.

"What happened?" the boy asked.

"Dracula bit her on the neck and got some of her blood."

"Why didn't they show it?"

"Because they didn't show that kind of stuff."

"Huh."

When the movie ended, the boy said: "Hey, what happened to Dracula?"

"Professor Van Helsing found the coffin where he sleeps and pounded a stake through his heart and killed him."

"When?"

"Just before the end."

Much of the censorial objection to *Frankenstein* (1931) centered on Fritz's (Dwight Frye) torture of and murder by the Monster (Boris Karloff). Frankenstein (Colin Clive) looks on.

"I didn't see that."

"No, they didn't show it."

"Why not?"

"I guess it's too scary."

A few minutes later, he heard the boy say to his mother, "It was kind of boring."

The next evening, they watched *Frankenstein*.

It reached the memorable scene when the monster has croaked the nasty hunchback, escaped from the castle, and tossed a girl into a stream.

"What happened to her?" the boy asked.

"She drowned."

"Couldn't she swim? She was only a few feet from the shore and it didn't look very deep."

"I guess not."

"Huh. Anybody can do the dog paddle."

The angry villagers were finally marching, torches aloft, to find the monster.

The man glanced at the boy. He was sleeping soundly.

In the morning, the boy said: "What happened to the monster?"

"He died."

"Yeah, I figured that would happen."

The mini-festival ended Sunday night with *Frankenstein Meets the Wolf Man.*

"How come there's never any color in these movies?" the boy asked.

"Because it is filmed in black and white."

"Oh."

When Lon Chaney Jr. turns into a hairy-face, the boy said: "Hey, cool."

But a few minutes later, he said: "What happened there?"

"He kills people by biting them on the neck."

"Why didn't they show that?"

"I told you, they didn't show graphic stuff like that."

The movie abruptly ended with a dam bursting and the floodwaters sweeping both creatures to wherever wet monsters and werewolves go.

The boy yawned and said: "Too bad. That Wolf Man was really a nice guy."

Then he said: "When you were a kid, you didn't really crawl under the seat in the movie theater, did you?"

"Uh, no, not really, unless I was looking for a lost glove."

"Yeah, I knew you were kidding."

"Yeah, sure I was."

It is, perhaps, a sad reflection on our times that movies which terrified audiences, outraged critics, and perplexed censors sixty years ago are now passé. However, this does not diminish the powerful effect the early horror films exerted. When seen through the eyes of their original audiences, critics and censors, the thirties' horrors were a fairly nasty lot. Although they shied away from actual bloodletting, these movies left few other stones unturned—and some repellent concepts occasionally slithered out.

The 1930s' "classic horror cycle" began with *Dracula* (1931) and could have ended there if the picture had not been a financial success. Censors (and "watchdogs" of public morality) were unprepared for the deluge of monsters that followed. Were these pictures harmful to audiences? Could

Lota (Kathleen Burke) and Parker (Richard Arlen), menaced by Dr. Moreau's "manimals" in *Island of Lost Souls* **(1933).**

children, especially, be damaged by seeing them? This argument continues—unsettled—to the present day.

One camp would have it that seeing graphic, ghastly doings on screen creates a catharsis, or cleansing, that renders the spectator incapable of committing the acts just witnessed. The other believes that violence seen is violence copied.

It's hard to see much sense in either position. Most horror fans would probably not admit to feeling especially "cleansed" after watching Bela Lugosi carve up Boris Karloff in *The Black Cat* (1934). Conversely, most viewers of the above don't carve up their companions after the movie ends. This brings us to the problem of censorship; must children and adults be protected from horrific films because of how they may or may not be influenced? This question is difficult to answer since movies that were once thought to be over the line are now miles behind it.

Gloria Holden gave censors more than just a feeling in *Dracula's Daughter*.

Although Mr. Royko's take on the subject is funny, there was no laughter among the thirties' film censors—especially in the United Kingdom. Pictures like *Frankenstein* (1931), *Freaks* (1932), and *Island of Lost Souls* (1933) outraged censors everywhere, but nowhere more so than in Britain.

The British Board of Film Censors, local watchdogs, and the clergy were uncertain about how to deal with the Hollywood horror invasion of 1932, and a five year war was waged to "protect" children from its influence. From their beginning, horror movies seem to have been made with a youthful audience in mind, the ideal patron probably being around fourteen or so. Adults were allowed as well, of course, but adolescents were more susceptible to the charms of *Frankenstein's Monster* and *Dracula.* This sort of thinking reached its peak with *I Was a Teenage Frankenstein* (1957).

The problems posed by children's exposure to and fascination with horror are many and not easily addressed, as the British found out. Due to the complex nature of the film censorship system, plus local "watch groups" fighting for their own autonomy, the British crusade to save children from Boris Karloff was alternatingly thought-provoking, infuriating, and absurd.

Their efforts culminated in making the exhibition of a "horrific" picture virtually impossible. This so-called "British Horror Ban" is often given "credit" for ending Hollywood's first horror cycle. This is true in a large sense; Britain *was* Hollywood's main importer, and it certainly did a studio little good to produce a picture that could not be shown in the UK.

However, by 1936, Hollywood producers (especially Universal) saw the future of horror and it was bleak. *Variety* (May 6) headlined "Horror Films Taken Off U Sked" (translation: Universal Schedule).

> Universal is ringing curfew on horror picture production for at least a year, following release of *Dracula's Daughter*, just completed. Latter will be released on current season's schedule, with no chiller pictures contemplated for 1936-37 release. Reason attributed by U for abandonment of horror cycle is that European countries, especially England, are prejudiced against this type of product. Despite heavy local consumption of its chillers, U is taking heed to warning from abroad. Universal has for a long time had virtual monopoly on this type of production, with unusual success at the box office. Studio's London rep has cautioned production exec to scrutinize carefully all so-called chiller productions, to avoid any possible conflict with British censorship.

No Hollywood studio had any "commitment" to the production of horror movies (or *any* type of movie)—only to making profits. When declining public interest in the genre combined with British censorship and bans, it was an easy decision to stop making horrifics. In some ways, the British ban of 1937 came too late; the horror movie was already dead.

While Britain has been singled out for its aversion to horror films, the situation existed in most countries—and it was not just a reaction against monsters. Unsavory sexual elements in the films, as much as anything, caused worldwide disapproval. Added to this mix was the public's saturation with horror: Between *Dracula* (1931) and *Dracula's Daughter* (1936), Hollywood produced close to forty horror movies, and not all of them were classics. It seems likely that the public simply grew weary of monsters and mad scientist movies, no matter how well or poorly they were done.

While it's easy to laugh at the labyrinthine maneuvering, contradictions, and jockeying for power that typified the British battle to protect children from unsuitable films, it was a necessary battle that is still being fought. These altercations which may appear to a modern reader as overreaction to any given thirties horror film were no less sincere than our current "V Chip" controversy over television violence. Sixty years have passed since the events in this book took place, and we *still* can't agree about what is fit for children to see—and about who is fit to decide.

As we despair over the violent attitudes and behavior of modern children, "the media" gets more than its share of the blame. In many ways, the situation remains unchanged from the thirties. One shudders at the thought of things to come.

Michael Medwin, in *Hollywood vs. America*, quoted David Puttnam, former president of Columbia Pictures:

> What we think of now as the excesses of the Roman circuses, where in the end hundreds of thousands of people died, didn't start that way. They started legitimately as circuses, extremely mild entertainment. But the audience's demand for more and more resulted over a period of several hundred years in that form of entertainment becoming more and more bloody, more and more grotesque. What might have been a woman raped publicly by a centurion, a year later was a woman raped publicly by an ass, and ten years later was ten women raped publicly by a hundred asses. The audience's desire for that goes back, deep into history. Someone has to say, "Enough," because this is a disaster—we are destroying ourselves.

If the author occasionally adopts what appears to be a position of moral superiority towards these movies, please be assured that is not the case; my own tastes run to the even more horrific (and disreputable) Hammer horrors of the fifties and sixties.

As a point of reference, my view towards the censorship of horror movies is that ax murderers are more likely created at home than in a theater. Still, it is possible that we've gone too far—but then, that's what they thought in the thirties.

A Brief History
of British Film Censorship

The British Board of Film Classification, in its 1995 Memorandum, is described as

> an independent, non-governmental body, which for over eighty years has exercised responsibilities over the cinema which by law belong exclusively to the local authorities. The licensing of cinemas was introduced by the Cinematograph Act of 1909, supposedly in order to ensure the physical safety of cinemagoers. Pubs and music halls were already licensed by the local councils, and the law now extended the powers to public cinemas as well, provided only that the conditions laid down by the license were reasonable ones. In 1911, the courts ruled that the prior censorship of films was a reasonable condition. The Board had been set up by the film industry in 1912 in order to bring a degree of uniformity to the standards of film censorship imposed by the many very disparate local authorities. The object was to create a body which, with no greater power than that of persuasion, would seek to make judgments which were acceptable nationally. To this end, the Board has needed to earn the trust of local authorities and also of Parliament, the press, and the public ever since. It must not only be independent, but be seen to be so, taking care, for example, that the film industry does not seek to influence Board decisions and that, similarly, pressure groups and the media are permitted to comment, but not to determine the standards set by the Board for the public at large. Statutory

9

powers remain with the local councils, who may overrule any of the Board's decisions on appeal, passing films we reject, *banning films we have passed*, and even waiving cuts, instituting new ones, or altering categories for films exhibited under their own licensing jurisdiction.

The Board has operated under the following set of guidelines since its inception:

• No film, other than a current newsreel, shall be exhibited unless it has received a certificate of the BBFC.
• No young people shall be admitted to any exhibition of a film classified by the Board as unsuitable for them, unless with the local authorities' permission.
• No film shall be exhibited if the licensing authority gives notice in writing prohibiting its exhibition on the ground that it "would offend against good taste or decency, or would be likely to encourage or incite to crime, or to lead to disorder, or to be offensive to public feeling."
• The nature of the certificate given to any film shall be indicated in any advertising for the film, at the cinema entrance (together with an explanation of its effect, and on the screen immediately before the film is shown).
• Displays outside the cinema shall not depict any scene or incident not in the film as approved.
• No advertisement shall be displayed at the premises if the licensing authority gives notice in writing objecting to it on the same grounds as apply to the prohibition of films.

Since, as previously stated, the BBFC is a non-governmental body, the above rulings were and are subject to the decisions of local authorities. London cinemas had additional conditions:

No film may be shown in London which is likely:
• To encourage or incite to crime.
• To lead to disorder.
• To stir up hatred against any section of the public in Great Britain on the grounds of color, race, or ethnic or national origins, or sexual orientation or sex.
• To promote sexual humiliation or degradation of, or violence towards women.
• To deprave and corrupt persons who are likely to see it, or

- Which contains a grossly indecent performance thereby outraging the standards of public decency.

The British Board of Film Classification, known colloquially as "Soho Square," began its rating system in 1913 with a simple two class system. A "U" (Universal) rating was given to a film specially recommended for children's matinee performances, and an "A" was given to a film more suitable for adults, "without the least implication that it might not be shown to children, for BBFC policy was that no film which was not 'clean and wholesome and above suspicion' should be given the sanction of any certificate at all."

Tom D. Matthews (*Censored*) revealed that the first film to be banned in Britain featured, as its "star," a piece of cheese! Charles Urban, an early film experimenter, shot through a microscope a section of blue-veined cheese. This blowup revealed bacteria in the cheese, and the British cheese industry campaigned vigorously against its exhibition, fearing the public's reaction. They won. This madness took place in 1898, and got the British film censorship system off to a start it would effortlessly maintain.

As Britain entered the Edwardian age, moralists and reformers were concerned (rightly as it turned out), about the negative influence of the cinema. Oddly, there was a great concern about the huge size of the projected image that made just about anything seem grotesque. Violence was more prevalent in films than sex in these early days, and would continue to be so in Britain until the seventies. Foreign producers, however, would not hesitate to supply the UK with all the prurient material it could handle.

Although films in the UK, as in America, would eventually be rented from distributors, in the beginning they were bought by the foot with neither stars or subject matter being considered; a foot was a foot. Audiences were so hungry for movies that practically anything would do—which made things easy for cinema bookers.

Large and ornate film palaces were constructed quickly; by 1911, there were almost 4,000. Movie viewing was largely the province of Britain's large middle class, and pictures were, at least in theory, made with their sensibilities in mind. The problem, naturally, was who was fit to decide what these sensibilities entailed.

One of the earliest examples of this was in 1910 when the London County Council banned the film of the heavyweight boxing championship bout between James Jeffries and Jack Johnson due to its violence.

The next year, the Blackburn Council decreed that cinema managers must permit the Council to screen pictures one week before their exhibition. Concerns were also voiced over the content of movie posters.

British film censorship officially began in January 1912 as an in-house program when Cecil Hepworth, a filmmaker himself, petitioned the Home Office to create a Board of Censors. The Board was to be financed by film producers' fees, and the HO was to be responsible for choosing a Head Censor. George Redford, formerly Chief Examiner of Plays, was given the position. Unfortunately, Redford's health failed almost immediately, and Joseph B. Wilkinson stepped in. Equally unfortunate was that Wilkinson had severe vision problems.

The British Board of Film Censors went to work in earnest one year after its inception, opening shop in Soho at 75 Shaftesbury Avenue. George Redford died in November 1916, and was officially replaced by T.P. O'Connor. By 1917, movies were already being blamed for crimes, especially those committed by children. In the 80 years since then, no one has yet been able to satisfactorily prove if that relationship does—or doesn't—exist.

During World War I, the BBFC's biggest burden was director Abel Gances' *J'Accuse!* This French antiwar classic featured soldiers killed in battle returning from the grave to question the justification of their deaths. This did not play well for the Board, which did not grant the picture a certificate. *J'Accuse!* finally opened in London, unrated, two years later.

In 1921, the London County Council adopted the BBFC certificate as a license requirement but stipulated that "no young person shall be admitted to be present at any exhibition at which films passed by the BBFC for 'Public' but not for 'Universal' exhibitions are shown, unless accompanied by a parent or bona fide adult guardian of such young person."

The LCC, in 1924, instituted an age restriction. "No 'A' film may be shown when a child or under 16 years is present, unless said child is accompanied by an adult (as in the 1921 ruling)."

The BBFC, it must be said, did not play favorites; even the silent era's most respected classics went under its scissors. Director Sergei Eisenstein's *Battleship Potemkin* (1926), due to its central sequence (the famous massacre on the Odessa steps), was banned for its "inflammatory working class rebellion" theme. Incredibly, the picture was not "legally" shown in the UK until 1954. Fritz Lang's *Metropolis* (1926), which carried a similar message, was cut to the point of being unrecognizable.

When sound pictures arrived, the British Board of Film Censors was not listening, and was unprepared for dealing with the new problems the new technology presented. Tom D. Matthews revealed that the Board felt "talkies" were a fad and never bothered to purchase sound equipment for its own use. Board members would watch the "silent" picture being reviewed while someone read the script aloud!

BBFC President O'Connor died in November 1929 and was replaced by Sir Edward Shortt, formerly Prime Minister Lloyd George's home secretary. It was under his watch that the Hollywood horror invasion of Britain began.

As a response to the horrors oozing out of Hollywood, a "horrific" category was instituted in 1932, but was "purely advisory." This was caused by the elusive nature of the horror film in general—*The Mummy* (1932), while technically a "horror movie," was certainly less violent, brutal, or terrifying than, say, *Public Enemy* (1931), or *Scarface* (1932). Since the horrific category did not place any enforceable restrictions on, or even identify a film as being a "horror movie," it was basically without purpose. An "H" *certificate* was instituted in 1937.

The "H" certificate was replaced in January 1951 by the "X," which was "not for merely sordid films dealing with unpleasant subjects, but films which, while not being suitable for children, are good adult entertainment and films which appeal to an intelligent public." As a result, thought-provoking adult dramas were placed in the same category as sex and horror movies.

In 1994, the Board took up a serious inquiry (again) into the nature of film violence and horror in hopes of determining the relationship (if any) between this type of entertainment and the commission of violent crimes. The results were, as one would expect, inconclusive.

> The first stage was a survey of the tastes and habits of young offenders between the ages of 12 and 17. Their patterns of viewing were compared to those of ordinary school children of the same age. The results were reassuring, but not conclusive, since we found they all watched very much the same films and programs. Even those with convictions for violent offenses had no particular viewing habits or preferences distinguishable from the group as a whole. What we could not yet determine was whether they interpreted the things they saw differently. The lives of the young offenders were sufficiently different from the comparison group of school children to raise questions about the meaning of violence for the two groups. For one thing, the social circumstances of the offenders were more deprived, their family back-

grounds more unstable. Many came from broken homes and reported fairly high levels of drug and alcohol use, perhaps to assuage feelings of depression or resentment at their chaotic lifestyles.

While certainly unscientific, one could reason that the above circumstances were also the case in the 1930s. If a certain group of people see a horror movie, whether it's *Frankenstein* (1931), *The Curse of Frankenstein* (1957), or *Mary Shelley's Frankenstein* (1994), each viewer brings to the picture his or her own social background, fantasies, and possible psychoses. It would seem that the viewer leaves the theater with the same problems he or she arrived with, and what happens or doesn't happen later has little to do with the movie he or she watched.

Children and Horror
Films in the U.K.

On March 6, 1933, the matter of "Children and 'A' Films" was addressed by the Home Office due to the frequency of underage audiences attending adult films. To ensure that parents were given every opportunity to know, in advance, the category of the film at the local cinema, a committee of the Home Office made the following recommendations:

- About 65 percent of cinemas in the UK were enforcing the "A" category, but only 40 percent were displaying the category notices. The committee felt that by raising the pitifully low 40 percent figure, parents would be forced to assume more responsibility for what their children saw.
- A periodic inspection of cinemas would be held to enforce the above.
- All cinema posters, to follow the BBFC guidelines, must advertise the category.
- An unexpectedly large number of children were persuading adults entering cinemas to sneak them into an "A" film. Cinema managers were threatened with the loss of their licenses if they permitted this abuse to continue.
- The Committee's "attention was drawn to a few unusually horrifying films which were particularly unsuitable for children. After reviewing these films, the Committee decided that, although they had been passed 'A' by the BBFC, some further action was desirable to ensure that parents were specially warned

15

A disturbing portrait of one of horror's most disturbing characters: Peter Lorre as Dr. Gogol in *Mad Love* (1935).

not to take young children to see them. The Committee discussed the matter with the Cinematograph Exhibitors' Association, who agreed to advise their members that when a film of this character is being shown, notices should be posted outside the cinema that the film is, in the opinion of the management, unsuitable for the children."

The secretary was deeply concerned about the content of movie posters, especially those advertising Hollywood horrors. In conjunction with the BBFC, a crackdown on "lurid" advertising was begun: "No poster, advertisement, sketch, synopsis, or program of a film shall be displayed, sold, or supplied either inside or outside the premises which is likely to be injurious to morality or to encourage or incite to crime or to be offensive to public feelings."

Despite the seemingly endless efforts of the British Board of Film Censors and the Home Office to protect Britons from Boris Karloff and Bela Lugosi, Hollywood kept pumping out horror movies, and the British (both adults and children) couldn't get enough.

On January 19, 1935, *The Times'* educational supplemental made public that, "A request for the appointment of a Government Committee to inquire into the conditions of administration in respect to the censorship of entertainment films was made to the Prime Minister by a deputation representing the National Cinema Inquiry Committee. The deputation was introduced by the Archbishop of Canterbury."

Clearly, the government felt that movies—and not just horror movies—were becoming a serious threat to public morality. Present at the inquiry were representatives from many areas of British life, with a heavy emphasis on religious and educational leaders.

The archbishop pointed out that British cinemas were attended each week by 20 million people, and many of them were children. While not wishing to reflect on the BBFC, he felt that too many "unsuitable" films were being exhibited and that too many children were seeing them. While not mentioning any specific type of film, the prime minister commented, "Any influence affecting children and young people must be regarded by all government as a matter of first-rate importance."

The Home Office secretary then, quite accurately, put his finger on the core of the problem. "It is difficult to reach a general agreement on matters largely of taste." What is considered acceptable in London may not be elsewhere, and since much of the censorship power was in the hands of local authorities, it must have been impossible to find a consensus.

How British Films Were Exhibited in the Thirties

Kenneth A. Nyman, in *Sight and Sound*, posed this question: Are films exhibited for profit or prestige? "Exhibitors, generally, realize that while they are in the business as entertainment caterers for profit, a constant study of the vagaries of public taste is essential for maintaining his profits; in his peculiar position of public purveyor he can, however, influence that taste and so increase the prestige of the business as well."

A cinema manager has a certain number of films to chose from, so should he or she book a film only for its profit-making potential, or should a higher goal be set? Just because a film has been passed for exhibition, Nyman pondered, does not necessarily mean that a showman is obligated to present it. So, what films should a manager seek out? What process was followed in the UK in the thirties before a movie was considered to be available for exhibition?

After a British or American-made film was submitted to the British Board of Film Censors, the following sequence of events was put into action. The BBFC either banned it (which routinely happened to a dozen pictures a year) or passed it: 1. For "universal exhibition" or "U" certificate; 2. For "public exhibition" or "A" certificate—no children permitted unless accompanied by a "responsible adult"; or 3. As "horrific" with an "A" certificate.

But, even if a picture was banned, it could still be exhibited in a specific area if local authorities chose to override the BBFC. It was not unusual to see film posters in the early thirties screaming, "Banned by Censors—Passed by _____ County Council!" This situation was almost exclusively associated with foreign-made films; British producers would routinely submit the script to the censor before beginning production.

The Film Act, then, specified that the picture be "trade shown," where critics and cinema managers had an opportunity to see the film privately. It was possible that a picture could be passed by the BBFC and trade shown, only to be later banned by a local authority (which also had the power to lift a BBFC ban).

After the trade show, the film was registered by the Board of Trade. A certificate was given, specifying its length and national origin. The picture was now eligible to be exhibited. It was then up to the exhibitor to determine if the movie was appropriate for its patrons. That determination was based on a number of factors, including star value, thematic suitability, possible offense to local religious or political views, depiction of some aspect of a patron's life in an unfavorable light, and the inclusion of offensive scenes of sex or violence.

Obviously, a cinema manger had many options to consider before exhibiting a film. Care had to be taken not to insult or upset one's regular patrons. With over 250 cinemas to choose from in greater London, a customer could easily take his business elsewhere.

A Brief History of
American Film Censorship

The censorship of American movies began soon after the advent of the nickelodeon when, in Chicago, a judge blamed the fledgling entertainment for inspiring juvenile crime. This link between movies and crime (juvenile or otherwise) has been an oft-leveled charge but is easier to contend than to prove. When similar complaints erupted in other large cities, the National Board of Censorship was created in 1909 to review—and, if necessary, cut—any film felt to be "unsuitable."

With the threat of government censorship looming, the film community felt that the best censorship was self censorship. As in the United Kingdom, local communities were given the power to decide what was "fit" for the locals to see. A Supreme Court ruling in 1915 denied movies—viewed as a business—the Constitutional protection of "free speech" enjoyed by newspapers, and the film industry became fairly diligent in policing itself.

When the twenties roared in following the end of World War I, America had become more "adult" and audiences—especially in large cities—demanded more "adult" entertainment. With movie stars behaving more scandalously both on screen and off, Hollywood quickly became a national symbol of decadence. Again, the industry took measures to police itself, forming the Motion Picture Producers and Distributors of America in December 1921. The goal was to instill "the highest possible moral and artistic standards into the film industry." Heading the MPPDA was Will Hays.

Hays had been a lawyer, a Republican National Chairman, and U.S.

Postmaster General. In 1930, the MPPDA (known as the "Hays Office") created the Production Code (which was soon known as the "Hays Code"). The Code strengthened Hays' 1927 ruling which outlined 11 "forbidden" topics (including nudity, drug abuse, sex perversion, and profanity). This earlier ruling generally demanded that the film industry present material that was in so-called "good taste."

The 1930 MPPDA was specifically concerned with two areas: sex and violence. Mae West ("Is that a pistol in your pocket or are you just glad to see me?") took care of the sex, while Boris Karloff and James Cagney provided the violence.

Religious groups were also up in arms, especially Catholics who, in 1934, formed the Legion of Decency as a result of years of protest by a committee of bishops. The Legion's purpose was not censorship per se, but rather to "warn" moviegoers about films of questionable content (and threaten the MPPDA). The Legion of Decency grouped movies into categories ranging from "A-1" (morally unobjectionable) to "C" (condemned). Little attention was paid to a picture's cinematic merit—all that counted was content. Most of the legion's power came from its ability to reach multitudes of Catholics who could be influenced to boycott "objectionable" films. To keep the Legion at bay, many Hollywood studios allowed the organization to screen their films before release for its "approval."

Under pressure from the Legion of Decency, other religious organizations, and local watchdog groups, the Production Code was stiffened on July 1, 1934. Its guiding principal was that "no picture shall be produced which will lower the standards of those who see it." A glance at the Hollywood horrors released prior to the new code (including *The Mask of Fu Manchu* and *Island of Lost Souls*) gives a good answer to why many felt a stricter code was necessary.

Dracula—*"The Strangest Passion the World Has Ever Known"*

Dracula (1931), of course, was not the first horror movie, but it is universally given credit for starting the sound horror cycle. The silent film era was awash with horrors, including the original version of *Dracula* filmed in Germany in 1922 as *Nosferatu*. The British Board of Film Censors had banned this classic, although not for its content. Bram Stoker's widow had successfully held on to the rights to her husband's novel *Dracula* up to that point and was not pleased with director F.W. Murnau's adaptation. She was quite vocal about her intention to sue anyone who infringed upon *Dracula*'s copyright and, to avoid possible litigation, the board chose not to give *Nosferatu* a certificate.

Oddly, despite well over 50 silents that could reasonably be classed as horrific in intention (if not in fact), few even today choose to see them as a unified group. This lot includes *Frankenstein* (1910), *The Golem* (1914), *The Picture of Dorian Gray* (1917), *The Cabinet of Dr. Caligari* (1919), *Dr. Jekyll and Mr. Hyde* (1920), *The Hunchback of Notre Dame* (1923), *The Hands of Orlac* (1924), *Waxworks* (1924), *The Phantom of the Opera* (1925), *The Cat and the Canary* (1927), *London After Midnight* (1927), and *West of Zanzibar* (1928).

These pictures contained most of the elements that would resurface in the 1931–36 cycle of horror movies, yet they apparently offended very few. The silent cycle lasted a quarter of a century, seemingly without seri-

The Count (Bela Lugosi) makes his move on Mina (Helen Chandler) in *Dracula* (1931).

ous controversy or censorship, yet the sound wave started by *Dracula* lasted a mere five years. But, what a five years!

Dracula had been a successful Broadway production, debuting on October 5, 1927, with Bela Lugosi in the lead. After many false starts (for both the studio and actor), the Universal film starring Lugosi finally began production on September 29, 1930. Lugosi's problem in getting the

Mina (Helen Chandler), the Count (Bela Lugosi), and Renfield (Dwight Frye) in a staged shot from the stage-bound *Dracula* (1931).

role was Lon Chaney, who had built a career on playing monsters. Universal's problem, after finally securing the rights to the property, was a fear of censorship.

Arthur Lennig (The Count) quoted several Universal "readers" about their fears concerning *Dracula*—fears far removed from vampirism. "It will be a difficult task, and one will run up against the censor continually," said one. "The first part of the story," opined another, "could be shown, but from the moment you take up the part of Lucy, you fall into all sorts of difficulties." A third took an even dimmer view. "Were this story put on the screen, it would be an insult to every one of its audience. We all like to see ugly things. But when it passes a certain point, the attraction dies, and we suffer a feeling of repulsion and nausea."

These memos were written in June 1927, and may have been instrumental in pushing *Dracula*'s production back three years. Considering some of the horrors that reached the screen prior to 1927, these trepidations seem excessive. In the end, it was not Bram Stoker's novel that was filmed, but rather the simplified stage version, perhaps in a final nod to the censor.

Renfield (Dwight Frye), a British estate agent, arrives at the Transylvanian castle of the mysterious Count Dracula (Bela Lugosi), despite being warned off by the locals. Dracula, a vampire, and his trio of undead "brides" terrorize the peasants who protect themselves with crosses and garlic. Dracula has summoned Renfield to help him purchase a house from which he can spread vampirism in England. The Count places Renfield under his power, transforming him into a fly-eating lunatic. After setting up residence, Dracula insinuates himself into the lives of Mina Seward (Helen Chandler), her fiancé John Harker (David Manners), Dr. Seward (Herbert Brunston), her father, and Lucy (Frances Dade), her friend. Dracula attacks and kills Lucy, and Professor Van Helsing (Edward Van Sloan) is called in to the case by Dr. Seward. Van Helsing suspects vampirism and that Renfield, an inmate in Seward's asylum, is somehow involved. Mina soon comes under Dracula's spell, and Van Helsing confronts the vampire with his knowledge. When Renfield escapes, Van Helsing and Harker follow him to Dracula's abbey, where the Count has imprisoned Mina. Dracula kills Renfield, but is destroyed by Van Helsing, who drives a stake through his heart before Mina is claimed as a permanent victim.

Universal was clearly concerned about the public's and critics' reactions after appeasing any potential censorship problems. The picture was released on Valentine's Day, 1931, as *The Story of the Strangest Passion the*

World Has Ever Known. Variety (February 18, 1931) felt that, "Such a treatment called for the utmost delicacy of handling because the thing is so completely ultra-sensational on its serious side, and the faintest excess of telling would make it grotesque." *The Los Angeles Times* (February 22) found *Dracula* "too extreme to provide entertainment that causes word of mouth advertising. Plainly a freak picture...."

After taking America by storm, Dracula next set his sights on London, which had been the vampire's original intention. There, in addition to fresh blood, he would meet two deadly adversaries: Van Helsing and the British Board of Film Censors. Although *Dracula* itself attracted little of the board's attention, the picture indirectly set into motion a national outcry for tighter censorship of films in general, and horror movies in particular.

"The problem," said Mr. S. Robinson, director of Ideal Films Ltd. (*Today's Cinema*, January 6, 1931), "is obviously going to be one of definition. What is sordid to one mind may not be sordid to another." Robinson was speaking about films in general, but his remarks certainly applied specifically to the coming wave of horror movies, beginning with *Dracula*.

The first sound adaptation of Bram Stoker's famous novel had opened—quite successfully—in the United States on February 14, 1931, and a trade show was scheduled for London's Prince Edward Theatre for February 18. "Universal's Fantastic and Fascinating *Dracula*!" screamed the British trade papers. "The Dead Who Lived on the Living! Awe Inspiring! Breathtaking! Heart Gripping! The Amazing Story of a Grotesque Passion!" No one yet seemed terribly upset with Bela Lugosi's bloodsucker.

Dracula was cut by about seven minutes before even being submitted to the BBFC, and received an "A" certificate with little difficulty. Relatively tame (some would say too tame) to begin with, *Dracula*, in this shortened form, also managed to avoid the wrath of local "watch groups" that would soon be attacking *Frankenstein*.

Dracula earned mostly positive reviews from the British trades, including *The Cinema* (February 25, 1931): "Universal and their clever technicians are to be congratulated on their adaptation of the famous Bram Stoker shocker. Especially we would commend the resourceful treatment of Tod Browning and the superb camera work of Karl Freund, for between them these two have ensured that atmosphere of brooding horror and well-nigh unbearable menace which were so characteristic of the book. Definitely, the picture is not for the squeamish, for all the dubious apologists which would seek to disarm their terrors at the end of the film. (Many) scenes, for all their faithful recapitulations of the book, are too repellently horrifying for any but the strongest minded, although the latter will agree that they have been given their money's worth."

The last sentence of this review would soon be amended—especially with the release of *Frankenstein*—to a far less positive tone.

By mid-March, *Dracula* was raking in so many pounds that few seemed to be upset by the picture's upsetting theme. "DRACULA'S BIG BUSINESS," announced a headline in *Today's Cinema* (March 17, 1931). "Crowds Turned Away from Opening Houses." *Dracula* was knocking them dead for a second time in London. "The opening was a showman's triumph," fawned *Today's Cinema*, "for not only was capacity reached and a long queue forced to wait round the Capitol Theatre block for hours, but hundreds were turned away. The remarkable scenes which marked the screen opening were a duplication of those which attended the first stage show years ago. Critics and managers had all looked pessimistically on the chances of Bram Stoker's thriller as a play. But from the sensational opening night, the play ran for over a year, and it is still playing around the country."

The same success was being predicted by the trades for Universal's film version. Crowds began forming at 3:45 P.M. for the 5:00 P.M. opening. "Any fears as to how the picture would go down were instantly washed away," enthused Jack Hart, the Capitol manager. "The packed house absorbed the picture and thrilled to its weird and eerie story. They enjoyed every minute of it." They must have—*Dracula* did a week's worth of business in three days. When *Dracula* moved to the New Victoria, it was proclaimed as the "sensation of the season," playing to standing-room-only crowds. Unfortunately for the fledgling horror genre, this "feel good" atmosphere would not last long in Britain (or in America, for that matter). Whether spurred on by *Dracula's* success or not, the push for tighter film censorship took off like a rocket in the vampire's wake.

The Cinema (March 18, 1931) spoke out against the rising tide and power of censorship groups. "Are Films Wicked?" asked a huge headline.

> The British Board of Film Censors have a strong objection to frankness—*on certain subjects*—because they believe that to say too much about those subjects is harmful. By the nature of their business, they are always looking for evil—and to suspect it in places where others—who do not spend their time looking for

evil—would never dream of finding it. The result of their year's hunt is PROUDLY DISPLAYED in the Annual Report. The number of ways in which films trespass against good taste—rape, the morals of the innocent—and besmirch the fair outlook of men and women makes an imposing list. But is it a list which does the film business any good? If the Censor's rule of thumb is "keep evil hidden," why do they not apply that rule TO THEIR OWN REPORT?

The editorial then attacked the Censor's attacks of films in general:

The Censors say that the horrible things we refer to have been cut out; therefore, the films shown are purged and clean. But— what effect will a list of those horrible things have on the minds of the many people who regard the screen as an evil influence? They will think—if such things have been cut out—WHAT OTHER EVILS HAVE BEEN LEFT IN?

They will say—the producers of films have tried to smuggle such horrible things into their films for innocent people to see. Their morals must be so bad that their work is NOT FIT TO BE SEEN.

The Censor objects to—suggestions of cruelty. Shakespeare did not.

The Censor objects to—severed human heads. The British Museum does not—severed human heads are on public display (and not marked "A" either).

The Censor's task is a difficult one. On the one hand, critics ask for more liberty of thought and expression. On the other hand, some people think the films already say too much. Whether that be the case or not, it cannot be good for the industry to blazon forth—in an UNCENSORED, UNEXPUR-GATED LIST—details of the many "wicked" things the Censor has found in films intended for public exhibition. Even though the wicked things prove—on examination—not to be so wicked after all.

Clearly, the British film industry was concerned about the rising tide of censorship and disapproval directed against movies in general. This puritanical movement was only the beginning, and would soon be directed towards specific types of films.

On April 7, 1931, the trades reported that, in 1930, the British Board of Film Censors had rejected 12 pictures and had "taken exception" to

191. The need for a "third certificate" to join the "U" and "A" was discussed, but no action was taken—which would so often be the case. This "third certificate" would eventually become the "H" for horrific films, and would lead to their banishment in the UK. While this was being discussed at the censor's office, *Dracula*, after smashing house records at the Capitol and New Victoria, did likewise at the Astoria.

The Sunderland Watch Committee, one of many local censorship groups that were multiplying like Dracula's victims, banned *Outward Bound*, "a gentle fantasy about life and death."

"It is an insult to religion," puffed a spokesman. "It is grotesque to caricature the Almighty in the way it is indirectly done by the 'Examiner' in this picture" (*Kinematograph Weekly*, April 18, 1931). This ban was lifted on June 5. Speaking for the picture was Alderman A. Barton: "The people must have freedom because if we do not we shall be at the mercy of a few who will act as censors of everything." Taking the dissenting view was Alderman J.G. Graves: "There is no limit in the direction of mental and moral degradation to which so-called purveyors of entertainment will not go for the sake of money." As events concerning television and movies in the nineties have proven, both were right.

Easy to miss among this talk of censorship was an announcement in the June 3, 1931, edition of *Daily Cinema*: Universal was to film Mary Shelley's *Frankenstein* and Edgar Allan Poe's *Murders in the Rue Morgue*.

On July 2, 1931, *The Cinema* revealed that Fox Film Corporation would cease production on "gangster films." Winfield R. Sheenan, vice president of production, cited a growing hostility directed toward this type of picture in both the United States and the UK. Carl Laemmle, president of Universal, was apparently either not listening or unconcerned; he announced on July 8 that "*Dracula's* box office success is so great that I believe there is a definite and exceedingly large public for the really horrifying thriller" (*Today's Cinema*, July 8, 1931). That said, Laemmle reported that production would begin immediately on *Murders in the Rue Morgue*.

A month later, the Southport Trade and Labour Party, a local watch group, passed a resolution against the exhibition of immoral films, and especially against children being permitted to see them. "Local authorities," said *The Cinema* (August 7, 1931), "were being urged to exercise their considerable powers of censorship." The Home Office secretary must have been listening—he advised the county councils to form a consulting committee and advise the British Board. Again under discussion was the mysterious "third certificate."

One immediate result of this discussion was an action taken against the Manor Picture House, Sheffield, in which 200 children were admitted to see Alfred Hitchcock's *Murder!*, in clear violation of the Cinematograph Act of 1909.

An innocuous notice appeared in the trades on September 30, 1931, announcing a "mystery story with a circus background." The picture in question was *Freaks* (1932), which would become, along with *Island of Lost Souls* (1932), among the most notorious of the early horrors. Both would be banned outright in the UK; *Freaks* would not be shown publicly (and legally) for 30 years.

Murder by the Clock (1931), a horrific mystery, incurred critical wrath of the kind avoided by *Dracula*. "A repellent story," sniffed *The Cinema* (October 3, 1931). "It is by no means a charming story nor are its gloom and horror lightened." *Dracula* was, officially, the only true "horror movie" in release at the time, but the indication was that more would follow, and both censors and critics were becoming wary.

The question of film certification again reared its ugly head when Liverpool banned children from "A" pictures, even when accompanied by a parent or adult guardian. Religious groups and child welfare organizations were behind the movement, which was upheld by a magistrate on October 16. The London County Council jumped in the next day, saying that it was "improper for a licensing authority to act *in loco parentis*." The council felt that parents should be, within limits, the final judge of what their children see and wanted to consult with the BBFC. Also at the October 17 meeting, a ban was placed on all Christmas and Easter screenings. Then on October 27, the LCC began looking at film posters for possible offensive material.

A bold step was taken by the BBFC on October 28, 1931, when one unnamed picture was given two certificates—an "A" in its original version, and a "U" after minor cuts. This seemed, at the time, to be the future of British film censorship: one film release in different versions for different age groups or geographic areas.

A move to strengthen the BBFC's position compared to local authorities was taken in early November. *The Cinema* (November 5, 1931) reported that, "The original rules were drawn up so many years ago and they have never been revised. Whereas the public outlook has definitely changed and has progressed toward more freedom of thought." R.V. Crowe, president of the Cinematograph Exhibitors' Association, felt that the existing "A" certificate should definitely rule out a certain class of film as being not suitable for children under any circumstances. This "certain class of film" would soon be making its way toward the UK. *The Cinema* announced (November 17) that *Frankenstein* would be arriving in London by the month's end and would be released in early May of 1932. *That* must have given the censors something to *really* think about.

Frankenstein— *The Movie That Made a Monster*

The potential censorship problems and adverse reactions to *Dracula* were minor when compared to those posed by *Frankenstein*. Although *Dracula* had helped bail Universal out of a serious financial dilemma, the studio was still having difficulties that only a major hit (or two) could solve. A new property for Bela Lugosi, now cast as the studio's savior, was sought. According to Greg Mank's *It's Alive!*, among the ideas discussed were "Grand Guignol" plays from the Paris stage, H.G. Wells' *The Invisible Man*, and Poe's *Murders in the Rue Morgue*. Leading the pack, though, was *Frankenstein*.

Mary W. Shelley's 1817 novel had met with its own censorship problems, and was finally published a year after its completion, as several firms refused to issue it. The first theatrical version, *Presumption or the Fate of Frankenstein* (1823), was plagued by picketers protesting against its blasphemous theme. Several film versions preceded Universal's but had no real impact; more important was Peggy Webling's London stage adaptation in 1927.

Originally planned as a Robert Florey–directed production with Lugosi as the monster, the Universal film quickly shifted into James Whale's hands on the strength of his *Journey's End* (1930). One of Hollywood's greatest legends has Lugosi ultimately refusing the role and Boris Karloff's "discovery" in the Universal canteen by James Whale. The story is also one of filmdom's most familiar.

Frankenstein (Colin Clive), with the help of the hunchbacked Fritz (Dwight Frye), creates a living being (Boris Karloff) from bodies of the

Fritz (Dwight Frye), Victor (John Boles), Elizabeth (Mae Clarke); and Frankenstein (Colin Clive) look on as Dr. Waldman (Edward Van Sloan) examines the Monster (Boris Karloff) in *Frankenstein* (1931).

dead. Due to Fritz's theft of an abnormal brain from Dr. Waldman's (Edward Van Sloan) classroom, the creature is born a psychopath. The monster ravages the countryside, drowning little Maria (Marilyn Harris) accidentally while playing a game. Frankenstein's wedding to Elizabeth (Mae Clarke) is interrupted by the monster, who is eventually hunted down and, presumably, killed in a burning windmill. Frankenstein, whom the monster had abducted, recovers and rejoins Elizabeth.

While considered pretty mild stuff today, *Frankenstein* was quite a shocker for its time. Although a huge box office success, the picture had many detractors on "moral" grounds and suffered significant cuts both before and during its release. The most infamous scene involves the monster and little Maria.

The two meet by a lake shore, and the child—strangely comfortable with the monster's appearance—contrives to play a game with him. She

P.D.926

Boris Karloff in *Frankenstein* (1931), with the shadow of Colin Clive.

hands him flowers, while throwing her own into the lake. "I can make a boat!" she laughs. "See how mine floats?" He follows her lead but, when his flowers are gone, makes a tragic mistake—he throws Maria into the lake. Karloff himself felt that scene was wrong, that the audience should *not*, at the very least, see the monster actually pick the child up and hurl her to her death. "I insisted on that part being removed," Karloff said (*Castle of Frankenstein* 9).

He eventually got his wish when, after a preview in November 1931, Universal president Carl Laemmle decided that drastic cuts were needed. Gone were the shots of Karloff grabbing the child; the scene ended with the monster reaching out for her. Unfortunately, this may have inadvertently implied an even worse fate for Maria.

Frankenstein opened at New York's Mayfair on December 4, 1931, as Universal held its collective breath. Although the picture was a small hit (breaking the Mayfair's house record), and received generally excellent reviews, problems were brewing. When *Frankenstein* premiered in Santa Barbara on December 6, there were many walkouts. Local censor boards struck hard, especially in Kansas where over 30 cuts were made before the movie could be shown. In several cities, newspapers declined to run advertisements.

The Hays Office, of course, was well aware that *Frankenstein* could post some serious problems while it was still in production. On August 8, 1931, Universal was notified that the office had concerns about "gruesome scenes that will certainly bring an audience reaction of horror." Specifically, these "gruesome scenes" included the body of a hanged man and Fritz's murder by the monster.

The real problem was that *Frankenstein* was a *horror movie* in every sense of the word. Of course, an audience would experience a "reaction of horror." That was why the picture was made and why people lined up to see it! If every horrific scene or concept was removed, *Frankenstein* would, obviously, no longer have been a "horror movie." Just as obviously, no one was being forced to see *Frankenstein* or any other horror film; the picture's advertising pulled no punches about its content, so it is doubtful that many paid to see the movie thinking it was a light comedy or musical.

When *Frankenstein* was released in Canada, the Quebec Censor Board rejected it in its entirety, but added a (ludicrous) condition: Universal could resubmit *Frankenstein* with a "preface to indicate the picture was a dream." Sweden and Italy were at least honest enough to ban *Frankenstein* unconditionally.

When Britain's Hammer Films unleashed *The Curse of Frankenstein* upon an unsuspecting public on May 2, 1957, the picture was greeted with a critical bashing almost as violent as the film itself. Critics in the UK seemed to take *The Curse of Frankenstein*'s horrific content personally. If only, many lamented, we could return to the good old days of the Karloff

Henry Frankenstein (Colin Clive) prepares to bring his creature to life as Fritz (Dwight Frye) looks on in *Frankenstein* (1931).

Frankenstein... Unfortunately, in their haste to trash the new version, the critics forgot (or, more likely, were unaware of) the savaging inflicted upon the old version.

Frankenstein was given a big play in the British trade press, as seen in *The Cinema* (November 11, 1931). "FRANKENSTEIN"—blared the headline—"More Amazing than *Hunchback* or *Phantom*...JAMES WHALE'S GREAT WORK...Famous British Artistes in Star Parts" (which must have come as a big surprise to the then-unknown Boris Karloff).

Boris Karloff, director James Whale, and stars Colin Clive and Mae Clarke were prominently pictured with Karloff—significantly—in a non-makeup pose. "Completing *Frankenstein*," *The Cinema* claimed, "has more than ordinary significance. No dramatic story of the season has relied so much upon the imagination and sympathetic understanding of its sponsors." A bit of flag waving soon surfaced. "The production is also notable for the fact that not only is its director an Englishman with a reputation, but Colin Clive (Dr. Frankenstein) and Boris Karloff (the monster) both hail from the Old Country."

Falling back on poetic license, *The Cinema* claimed that, "During the one hundred years Mrs. Shelley's novel *Frankenstein* has been constantly in publication and circulation, no edition of the work has appeared with illustrations. No artist has ever had the temerity to depict the features of the 'monster' which Dr. Frankenstein created; no pen or brush has brought to life the eerie and fantastic creation."

The trades were predicting great things from *Frankenstein*, which Mr. S.F. Ditcham, Universal's managing director, proclaimed as "The Picture of 1932." It is difficult to reconcile this enthusiastic reporting of *Frankenstein* as a major cultural event with the events that soon followed.

On November 4, 1931, *The Kinematograph Weekly* announced that a closer cooperation between the British Board of Film Censors and local authorities would be encouraged to "produce greater uniformity." It was agreed that "local licensing would be finally responsible for the character of films shown to the public." The split between the two would never really close, as *Frankenstein* soon pointed out. Pictures passed by the BBFC would be shown in one town and banned in the next. The next day, R.V. Crowe, president of the Cinematograph Exhibitors' Association, proposed (not for the last time) a "third certificate" to supplement the "A" and "U."

"*Frankenstein* will arrive in London before the end of the month," warned *Today's Cinema* (November 17, 1931), "with a release date set for May 2, 1932. Weird, uncanny, the great thrill of your life!"

Nineteen hundred thirty-two opened with "SERIOUS CENSORSHIP MOVES" (*Today's Cinema*, January 6) in the UK. Two pictures, *Stepping Out* and *Why Change Your Husband?* were banned and removed from the Plaza and the Carlton. Incredibly, *Dracula* moved into the latter! Cinema owners were on shaky ground as the "A" certificate was keeping adults home in droves, since they could not take their children with them. "The increasing interference of the local authorities," opined *The Cinema*, "in a matter which they were previously content to leave to the BBFC, threatens to have a serious effect on the industry."

A small notice also appeared that day, announcing that Tod Browning "may have the greatest aggregation ever assembled of human monstrosities for *Freaks*." But, the British public would not see the soon-to-be-banned picture for 30 years.

Universal planned to tie its 1932 UK releases together under a literary banner. "New Year's Big Start with *Frankenstein*," proclaimed *Today's Cinema's* (January 6) headline. "Authors include Wells, Stevenson, Edgar Allan Poe, and Mary Shelley. Wide Variety of Fare from Plays, Books." Boris Karloff was proclaimed the successor to Lon Chaney as "*Frankenstein* is breaking records with top admission prices all over the United States." No mention was made of any opposition to the picture, but quite a bit was said about Universal's upcoming *Murders in the Rue Morgue* and *The Invisible Man*.

Frankenstein began creating controversy in the UK long before its release. An organization called "The Order of the Child" was making its move—through contacts with the Cinematograph Exhibitors' Association—to address *Frankenstein*'s exclusion from being on children's viewing menus. "To show a film like *Frankenstein*—if it is what I hear it is—under the ordinary 'A' certificate is to place a weapon in the hands of the people who are agitating for the complete exclusion of children," said the secretary of the CEA. "It is particularly a case in which a third certificate would be to the benefit of the trade and public alike." The National Society for the Prevention of Cruelty to Children began pressuring the BBFC to introduce an "H" (horrific) advisory. This, when it was finally instituted, did not immediately become effective. For example, *Vampyr* (1931) was finally exhibited without cuts in May 1933, bearing an "H" despite being even more tame than *Dracula*. Pictures far more horrific than *Vampyr*—*Murders in the Rue Morgue* and *Mystery of the Wax Museum*—were certified as "A." *Freaks*, which at least carried a moral, was banned outright in July 1932.

"*Frankenstein*," continued the secretary, "has been specially designed for adults, but it would be a great pity if the present censorship arrangements should allow a film of this caliber to be used for propaganda purposes against the liberty of parents to decide which pictures their children should see" (*The Cinema*, January 7, 1932).

In Beckenham, the local council banned children under 16 from seeing an "A" picture even if accompanied by a parent, following a motion made in Liverpool.

Exhibitors were becoming frightened at this potentially catastrophic loss of revenue and planned to petition Parliament. The Beckenham move was sponsored by the town's education committee, which argued, quite reasonably, that if a movie is "unsuitable" for children, it makes little difference if the child's parents also watch it. A similar ban in Sheffield was lifted before being enacted due to media and public pressure. As various groups argued over a parent's right to decide what movies their child could see, the UK grew a step closer to a "third certificate."

Carl Laemmle, Universal's president, wrote a weekly column in *Today's Cinema*, and his January 11, 1932, effort sang the praises of *Frankenstein*. "Universal is mighty proud of this masterpiece ... the direction is nothing short of the work of genius; Colin Clive ... lives and breathes the role of Frankenstein ... and Boris Karloff—mark his name well! *Frankenstein* is the greatest hold-over picture ever produced." But, as *Frankenstein* neared its UK release, few could have imagined the firestorm Laemmle's masterpiece was about to ignite. By exposing Britain's ludicrous censorship situation and questioning parental supervision of children, *Frankenstein* had truly created a monster.

At that time, cinema owners were more frightened of the Beckenham decision that they were of the Frankenstein monster. *The Kinematograph Weekly* (January 12, 1932) feared that the "Beckenham Rule may spread," and that it was a "threat to exhibitors." *Today's Cinema* (January 12) opined, "The setting up of a local censorship panel is likely, in the long run, to cause even more embarrassment to the trade than the 'Liverpool Rule.' It is a policy which is very likely to be adopted ... and the result will be that no exhibitor will know how he stands with a particular film until he has booked it and the local panel has seen it."

Another gaunt monster reared its ugly head—fear that America's Depression would destroy the movie industry was spreading through Britain. "Conditions in the States are very bad," said Sam Morris of Warner Brothers, "and were not getting any better at the time I left." This was one more thing for British exhibitors to worry about—less product.

There was *one* American picture, at least, ready to be shown: *Frankenstein* was set to premiere at the Tivoli on January 25. "*Frankenstein* has already broken box office records all over the states," bragged *The Cinema* (January 15, 1932), "and is playing in runs extended as long as a month in cities where one week is general."

With *Frankenstein*'s premiere ten days away, the CEA petitioned the British Board of Film Censors to create a third certificate for films unsuitable for children. Due to the constant intervention of local watch groups, the CEA felt that a nationally binding decision was necessary to protect cinema owners.

"*FRANKENSTEIN*—Universal's Grand Guignol of the Screen" blared a *Kinematograph Weekly* headline (January 20, 1932). "Macabre Thriller Which Will Make Money." At an exclusive press showing, *Frankenstein* impressed the crowd: "It touches the highest peak of sensational melodrama. That it will make money for the popular showman is undoubted, though its uncompromising depiction of stark horrors and gruesome experiment are calculated frankly to appeal to the unsqueamish."

Today's Cinema (January 21, 1932) called *Frankenstein*, "very free and modernized adaption. Scenes which for sheer horror were unexcelled on screen and rouse pity and fear ... direction emphasizes gruesome nature of theme ... box office fare for showmen but not family fare ... powerful portrayal by Boris Karloff in one of the most difficult roles possible to imagine ... so hungry is the public for entertainment which will transport them far from everyday life that we find it difficult to predict other than extraordinary success."

Coincidentally, as *Frankenstein* was presented to a quavering British public, a cry went up for a national censor, which would negate the local committees.

Today's Cinema (January 23, 1932) led with the one-inch headline "ATTACK ON *FRANKENSTEIN*." The Order of the Child, the CEA, the Tivoli Cinema, and the London County Council all huddled over *Frankenstein*. F.B. Kirby, the Order's secretary, said he had not yet seen *Frankenstein* and was basing his views on press releases, but would see the picture in a few days and would withdraw any objections if he was wrong. "We do not want to interfere with the prerogative of parents to take children to see 'A' films. That being so, there is obviously a case for a third certificate, and this is one of them. There are thoughtless people among parents who do not study the child's point of view and we are going to do our best to see that no child sees this picture." In a letter to the manager of the Tivoli, Mr. Kirby asked, "Might I express the earnest hope of my committee that it is your intention to take definite action to exclude children from performances of this film?" The LCC was given copies of all correspondence from the Order.

Gaumont British, which owned the Tivoli, reacted by displaying, "In Our Opinion, This Film Is Unsuitable for Children" on all *Frankenstein* advertising, plus inside the cinema's vestibule, if any child got that far. "We have made our point," said Kirby. "It is now up to the trade."

Seemingly oblivious to its own controversy, *Frankenstein* opened at the Tivoli on Monday, January 25, 1932, to "Impressive Box-Office Takings" (*Today's Cinema*). Colin Clive joined an array of industry dignitaries as a huge crowd outside waited in vain for admission.

Meanwhile, the Beckenham town council rejoined the action, revealing an attitude that was, according to the trades, "out of tune with public opinion."

Despite the reservations of censors, local watch groups, and spoilsports, audiences and serious film critics loved *Frankenstein*. A sampling of quotes in *Today's Cinema* on January 29: "The most sensational motion picture ever made" (*Sunday Times*); "Good sensationalism and good art" (*London Times*); "An outstanding film" (*The Star*); "A good scream and a faint never did anyone any harm" (*Daily Telegraph*); "You've got to admit it's good" (*Empire News*); "Brilliant to the point of genius" (*Daily Dispatch*); "Brilliant, mordant, vivid" (*Daily Sketch*); and "The most talked of picture among the new West End shows" (*Daily Mirror*).

As critics raved and censors railed over *Frankenstein*, Universal planned to open *Murders in the Rue Morgue*. S.F. Ditcham, managing director, pointed out that, "Universal is losing no time in completing their cycle of eerie pictures." Perhaps Carl Laemmle saw the end of the cycle as it was just beginning; he could hardly have been unaware of the rising tide of anti-horror factions in both the United States of America and the United Kingdom.

Ireland joined the fray when Belfast's Film Committee of the Churches announced on February 9, 1932, that it felt *Frankenstein* should be banned, despite the fact that no committee member had actually *seen* the film. A local paper had called *Frankenstein* "a shocker," and that was good enough for them.

Taking a break from bashing *Frankenstein*, the Beckenham council next attacked *The Gorilla*, better known in its 1939 version with the Ritz Brothers, Bela Lugosi, and Lionel Atwill. The council warned exhibitors that, in the future, children would not be admitted to "A" films unless the censors could see the picture ten days in advance. As for the gorilla, Rev. R. Burges said, "Even grown up people would be afraid of it" (*Today's Cinema*, February 16, 1932). "Without seeing even half of the film, I had made up my mind that it was not fit for children. I cannot understand the taste of people who make films like this."

The Irish Free State, in opposition to the position taken by Belfast, praised *Frankenstein*: "Karloff's interpretation is worthy of a place amongst the greatest pieces of film work ever done. It is a marvelous film" (*Dublin Evening Herald*, March 28, 1932). "The picture has its gruesome moments, but on the whole, praiseworthy restraint has been exercised." Less than a month later, Belfast's Classic Cinema was ordered by police action to stop exhibiting *Frankenstein*. Following a complaint made by city churchmen, police ordered a special showing on April 20. Following a screening, a 3-2 vote was taken to ban the picture. S.F. Ditcham, Universal's man on the scene, was stunned, since the Irish censor had passed *Frankenstein*.

On April 26, 1932, *Today's Cinema* reported that even the private showing for the police should not have been allowed. Proper channels had not been followed, and all concerned with the screening were now in violation of the Irish code. The farce continued, when, on April 27, the Belfast Police Committee gave Universal permission to screen *Frankenstein* to city cinema owners and members of Parliament. All that was really accomplished by this was to point out the absurdity of the system.

The system, however, won; the police veto was permitted to stand by the Belfast Corporation, and cinema owners voiced their displeasure. The entire film trade in Belfast was in jeopardy due to the sloppy, seemingly formless procedure of the Police Committee. The public was against the ban, as witnessed by over 50 letters of protest to local papers received by May 4. A lone voice of reason was raised by Alderman Pierce, who had actually *seen Frankenstein* and felt that there was nothing wrong with it and that it taught a great lesson. "Don't prove yourselves to be a lot of imbeciles by supporting the action of the Police Committee, who should not censor films," he said to his colleagues (*Today's Cinema*, May 4).

Alderman Alexander countered by calling *Frankenstein* not immoral but "unmoral," and felt it was not entertaining, but "disgusting," and was not fit for "normal" people to view.

A cautionary note was sounded by Councillor J. Boyle. "If we go on with the ban, we will drive away any hopes of the cinema trade proceeding with its plans in Northern Ireland. If they knew that pictures were going to be banned after being passed by the censor in London, they would not have any encouragement to go on with their plans, and thus there would be increased unemployment in Belfast."

The final word in this absurd situation is almost beyond belief; *Frankenstein* was playing out a problem throughout the rest of Northern Ireland including Lurgan, which borders on Belfast. But, *Frankenstein* was banned to children in Birmingham on May 6, in Plymouth on May 10, and Leicester on May 11.

Not only was *Frankenstein* being indiscriminately banned, but cuts were being made at the whim of local groups. When the Plymouth Watch Committee excised the famous scene of the monster drowning little Maria, S.F. Ditcham had had enough. Universal's beleaguered managing director filed a "vigorous protest" against the cut.

> I cannot let the occasion go without the strongest protest on behalf of this company, as well on behalf of the exhibiting industry. The action in Plymouth in eliminating the scene ... is entirely misguided though, no doubt, well intentioned. When the picture came up for discussion by the BBFC, special reference was made to the scene in question. It was decided that this scene should necessarily be retained in the film, as it is the one sequence in the picture in which a human side is revealed in the makeup of this machine-made man. Yet, this great scene must not be shown to Plymouth audiences. The monster must remain a monster, without a soul, without human emotions, without a saving grace, throughout the entire film. I would remind exhibitors that the Censor Board gave the most careful consideration to *Frankenstein*, as it does to all films. I admit the Board deleted certain footage; but in doing so, its members ... gave an approval for the public showing of the film which guaranteed a standard of decent entertainment.

Ditcham felt that, since the BBFC had *already* cut the film, it proved that the drowning scene deserved to be seen by *all* audiences. The Plymouth Watch Committee, in his view, had no right to delete what the BBFC had passed. This would be a recurrent problem faced by horror movies. Individual scenes—if not entire movies—that had been passed nationally would be slashed by local watch groups.

Under the British censorship rules of 1932, there was no appropriate way to deal with *Frankenstein*. When it played at the Regent in the resort town of Bournemouth, the film was "one of the biggest winners—it attracted huge crowds on the Whitsun holiday" (*The Kinematograph Weekly*, May 26, 1932). This aside, the Regent's manager made it clear that *Frankenstein* was not suitable for children. The Nottingham Watch Committee passed the picture for "audiences of sixteen years or older." Max Corne, manager of the Cardiff New Imperial, wired Universal that *Frankenstein* had broken all house records, including an incredible 3,648 paid admissions in one day

Colin Clive as Henry Frankenstein, whose monster created a censorship nightmare in *Bride of Frankenstein* (1935).

(*Today's Cinema*, May 28, 1932). Police had to be called, he said, to control hundreds of people who were turned away. The Regent, Sheffield, reported over 21,000 admissions in a three-day period, which set yet another record.

James Welsh, vice president of the Cinematograph Exhibitors' Association, addressed "Censorship" at the June 2, 1932, session. "The problem of censorship," he said (*Today's Cinema*, June 3), "in connection with cinema films is one that is always likely to exist in some form or another. No censorship can hope to satisfy all the critics. It is frequently suggested that each locality should censor films for themselves, but if the present partial method adopted in some towns is to be taken as a model, then few would consider it satisfactory. No one can pretend that the present method of dividing the films into two categories is an ideal solution, but it does serve some purpose by indicating the need for caution on the part of the parent. It is the duty of the parent to decide on the nature of the entertainment suitable for the child."

As if to prove Welsh's point, the Preston Watch Committee banned *Frankenstein* three days later, claiming that its exhibition was not in the public interest, was not suitable for children, and was gruesome in its details. By June 12, Preston audiences had found *Frankenstein* playing down the road in Southport and were happily flocking to see it.

The clergy in Tunbridge Wells was the next to attack *Frankenstein*, doing so from the pulpit. Unfortunately, the result was an increase in attendance at the local cinema. Rev. Brockbank felt that advertising which banned children was not enough. The manager of the Opera House Cinema countered with, "There is a perfectly efficient censorship which passes or rejects all films, and as *Frankenstein* was passed by the censor, he at least saw nothing in it which would prove harmful. The best judges of what is good or bad are the public, and believe me, they will taboo a picture if it is in any way harmful" (*The Kinematograph Weekly*, June 30, 1932).

No other horror movie would generate both the box office and the bashing as did *Frankenstein*. Although the genre would continue strongly for another four years, in some ways it ended—at least in the UK—in the morass of contradictory censorship heaped upon *Frankenstein*.

The Sons of Frankenstein—
"I'll Show You
What Horror Means"

Murders in the Rue Morgue (1932) is best remembered today as the picture Universal handed to director Robert Florey and star Bela Lugosi after both lost out on *Frankenstein*. After directing Lugosi in a legendary—and lost—20-minute test reel, Florey was removed when James Whale bumped him. Lugosi then gave himself the worst break of his luckless career when he chose not to play the monster and was replaced by Boris Karloff (in more ways than one). Florey and Lugosi were so on reunited when *Murders in the Rue Morgue* began production on October 18, 1931. The behind-the-scenes intrigues and bad career moves obscure the film's true claim to fame: it contains one of the most perverse scenes in horror film history.

Dr. Mirakle (Bela Lugosi), committed to his "mad theory" of evolution (which predated Charles Darwin's), exhibits Erik, a trained ape, at a carnival in 1845 Paris. Erik is attracted to Camille (Sidney Fox) and snatches her bonnet as she and Dupin (Leon Waycuff) stroll by. After sending Janos (Noble Johnson), his servant, to follow Camille, Mirakle rescues a prostitute (Arlene Francis) from a street brawl. He takes her to his laboratory where he again attempts to prove a kinship between man and ape by "mixing their blood." Like those before her, she dies, and her body is dumped into the Seine. Dupin, investigating the killings, discovers a mysterious ingredient in the victim's blood when her corpse is fished from the river. He begins to suspect Mirakle after learning he has sent Camille a new hat. When he is refused entry to her apartment, Mirakle sends Erik in through a window. The ape kills Camille's mother (Betsy Ross Clarke), stuffs her corpse up the flue, and abducts the girl. Dupin and the Prefect (Brandon Hurst) arrive at the lab in time to prevent the "blood mixing." Mirakle is killed by the confused Erik, who is shot from a rooftop by Dupin.

Edgar Allan Poe has proven to be a difficult author to adapt for movies, and the script by Tom Reed and Dale Van Every has little to do with the original other than the "flue-stuffing." What it *does* have are several scantily clad harem dancers. "Do they bite?" asks a dirty old man. "Oh yes," replies his equally dirty old friend. "But you have to pay extra for that." Gazing at the same young women, Camille muses, "See how brown they are. Is that their real color, or have they painted themselves?" Dupin smirks, "Shall I find out for you?"

Dialogue like this, plus the picture's emphasis on evolution and a knife fight over a streetwalker's "favors" must not have played well among church groups, but these were minor compared to a scene with something to offend everyone.

"We shall see if you will be the Bride of Science?" intones Mirakle to the prostitute who is trussed up in a crucifixion pose. After checking her blood under a microscope, Mirakle is disgusted. "Rotten blood," he wails. "You … your blood is rotten—black as your sins. You cheated me. Your beauty was a lie!"

Then, incredibly, Mirakle falls to his knees, head bowed and hands clasped as if in prayer, before the syphilitic, crucified hooker!

Murders in the Rue Morgue is usually dismissed, even by fans of the Universal classics. Lugosi's performance is likewise—and unfairly—made sport of by many. Actually, the role is at least as well-acted as Lugosi's more oft-praised Dr. Vollin in *The Raven*, and is one of the actor's creepiest. The *New York Times* (February 11, 1932) was not impressed with either Lugosi or the movie: "Poe, it would seem, contributed very little. … It is not in any important respect to be confused with Poe's detective story. What is it that Bela Lugosi, who fulfills the role of Dr. Mirakle, is trying to prove with his blood tests remains … a matter of conjecture. The entire production suffers from an overzealous effort at terrorization."

The *Times'* sharp-eyed reviewer, however, was unable to spot the picture's questionable taste and pro-evolution stance. It is hard to believe that the *Times* would criticize *Murders in the Rue Morgue* for straying from its source, yet not bat an eye at its considerable excesses.

Dr. Mirakle (Bela Lugosi) and Erik in *Murders in the Rue Morgue* **(1932).**

Dr. Mirakle (Bela Lugosi), the streetwalker (Arlene Francis), and Janos (Noble Johnson) in one of the decade's sickest scenes in *Murder in the Rue Morgue* **(1932).**

The British trades announced *Murders in the Rue Morgue* two weeks before *Frankenstein*'s London premiere. Under the headline "SCREEN SHOCKS!" *Today's Cinema* (January 6, 1932) enthused, "Edgar Allan Poe is another name to conjure with in the realm of the mysterious and romantic; here again, Universal has scored a success by selecting *Murders in the Rue Morgue*."

Lugosi and his ape arrived in London the first week of February, "indicating that Universal is losing no time in completing their cycle of 'eerie' pictures." (*Kinematograph Weekly*, February 4, 1932). Lugosi's Dr. Mirakle was described as "an even more menacing figure than Dracula"—and, in many ways, he was. Paramount's *Dr. Jekyll and Mr. Hyde* was trade shown, to excellent reviews, that same week. Both movies contain more than their share of violent and risqué material and were probably spared from heavy censorial attacks due to the heat taken by *Frankenstein*.

Like *Dracula* (1931) and *Frankenstein* (1931), *Dr. Jekyll and Mr. Hyde* (1931) was based on a famous literary source; indeed, Robert Louis Stevenson's 1886 novella was one of the most respected and dissected works of its period. The story was first dramatized in 1887 with Richard Mansfield in the lead(s). Mansfield became as closely identified with the roles as Bela Lugosi would be with Dracula. In 1908, Thomas E. Shea was filmed during a stage performance in the first of many cinematic treatments. John Barrymore starred in the first "real" version in 1920, pulling off a stage-like effect by transforming more or less without elaborate makeup or camera effects.

As one of the earliest horror movies, the Barrymore version left critics confounded—as many would be by the later remakes. Burns Mantle wrote in *Photoplay* (June, 1920):

> I have a friend ... who insists ... that *Dr. Jekyll and Mr. Hyde* gave her a most terrific attack of the movie blues from which she has not yet recovered nor expects ever fully to recover. Its very excellence as an acted horror has set her advising all the mothers she knows to keep their children away from it and to guard themselves accordingly.
>
> Frankly, I do not care for horrors, either on screen or stage. If they possess a soul-purging virtue that does us good, it must work subconsciously in my case.
>
> It will easily become the most talked of picture of the time. A door and two windows were broken by the crowds that tried to see it on its first showing in New York. The curiosity to see it will be great. But as to its continuing popularity, I have my doubts.

However, Fredric March pretty much laid claim to the roles with his Oscar winning performance for Paramount in 1931, which remains, justifiably, the best known version.

Dr. Henry Jekyll (March) believes that man is actually made of two selves which, if they could be separated, would result in the "good" self being freed. He is almost right.

Jekyll has been denied marriage to Muriel (Rose Hobart) by her stuffy father (Halliwell Hobbs) who insists that the doctor wait a "decent" period. On the way home from a party at Muriel's, Jekyll and his friend Lanyon (Holmes Herbert) break up a fight between two prostitutes.

Muriel (Rose Hobart) assaulted by her lover's alter-ego (Fredric March) in *Dr. Jekyll and Mr. Hyde* **(1932).**

Jekyll is overcome by Ivy's (Miriam Hopkins) charms, and is disgusted by his weakness.

In his laboratory, Jekyll downs a drug designed to free his "better" nature, but his evil side, Mr. Hyde, is released. Hyde is a near Neanderthal who sexually abuses Ivy before finally murdering her.

When Hyde finds himself unable to transform back to Jekyll, he enlists Lanyon's help to get the needed drugs. Lanyon insists on knowing the truth, and is horrified when he learns it. Jekyll decides to give up Muriel, but Hyde asserts his power and nearly kills her. Escaping from her home, Hyde murders her father and hides in Jekyll's laboratory. Transformed back into Jekyll, he is apparently safe, but is given away by Lanyon. Out of control, Hyde reappears and is shot by a policeman, and the monster's corpse reverts to that of Jekyll.

Directed by Rouben Mamoulian with abundant visual flair, the film was a showcase for all concerned. *Dr. Jekyll and Mr. Hyde* is best remembered today for, in addition to March's fine acting, Mamoulian's ingenious transformation scene involving complex lighting and camera filters. What gave the picture its initial notoriety, though, was sex.

Sex may not have been heavy on Robert Louis Stevenson's mind when he wrote the story, but it certainly preoccupied its many cinematic adaptors. This interest in Jekyll/Hyde's sex life reached its peak (or nadir) in Hammer's *The Two Faces of Dr. Jekyll* (1960), in which a burnt-out, middle-aged Jekyll becomes a young, handsome sex maniac as Hyde.

Mamoulian and writers Samuel Hoffenstein and Percy Heath saw Hyde as man at his most basic, interested mainly in his own animalistic needs. What is denied to the gentlemanly Jekyll was all too available to the unrestrained Hyde. The monster's sadistic baiting and beating of the unfortunate Ivy must have been quite an ordeal for 1931 audiences; it's shocking enough today, and presents a dictionary definition of sexual harassment.

In what must be one of the most harrowing scenes of its time, Ivy sits in her room with her landlady, discussing Hyde's domination of her, sexual and otherwise. "If that blighter was *my* man," the old woman says, "he wouldn't dare to lay a hand on me. Not if he knows what's good for him. And my advice dearie…"

Hyde enters the door, glaring at the women. The landlady's courage melts instantly and she slinks out. As he brutally questions Ivy, she begins to fall apart. Grabbing her bruised arm, he lisps, "You aren't lying to me, are you, my little bird? If I ever catch you lying, these are a trifle to what you'll get … *a trifle!*" Hyde makes himself at home with Ivy's newspaper and notices that Muriel and her father have returned to London after a month's absence. "Come here!" he growls. "Sit down, so that I can look at you, my sweet thing. Say it aloud—don't you think I can read your thoughts, you troll? You hate me don't you? I'm not a nice, kind gentleman like…"

He kneels at her feet, his face against hers. "Tell me you hate me—please my lamb—please my dear sweet pretty little bird. Tell me you hate me." Ivy stammers, "I don't know what you mean." "Then if you don't hate me, you must love me. Ahh ... how you must love me. I want to hear you say it—say it—come my love, *say it!*" He presses his face to her breast, telling her that he has some "bad" news—he is going away for a few days. Ivy inadvertently smiles. He jerks his head quickly to catch her. "Upon my word if you don't seem pleased. But pleasure is brief in this world my sweet, and yours is most uncertain because you don't know when I'll be back. If you do one thing I don't approve of while I'm gone—the least little thing, mind you—I'll show you what horror means!"

Hyde kisses her breast. "I'm not going now—I'm going to spend the evening with you. The last evening is always the sweetest.... What a farewell this one will be!"

It was certainly enough for the *New York Times* (January 2, 1932): "The producers are not a little too zealous in their desire to spread terror among audiences." *Variety* (January 2) concurred: "a high pitch of emotional horror." The scene described above, and several others, probably could not have been filmed outside of a horror movie; if Hyde were just an "ordinary man," the scene would be unbearable in its realism.

The Hays Office had many concerns about *Dr. Jekyll and Mr. Hyde's* dialogue, in addition to its horrific visuals. Chief among the offending lines was Ivy's to Hyde: "Take me." Hyde responded: "I'm going to take you!" Col. Jason S. Joy, director of the Studio Relations Office of the Association of Motion Picture Producers, called the dialogue, "Not only brutal, but suggestive.... Because the film is based on so well established a literary classic, the public and the censors may overlook the horrors which result from the realism of the Hyde makeup." In a December 5, 1931, memo to the Hays Office Joy tellingly wrote, "Is this the beginning of a cycle which ought to be retarded or killed?" The "horror cycle," only in its infancy, had already been identified as such—and already identified in some quarters as being undesirable.

The British trades treated *Dr. Jekyll and Mr. Hyde* respectfully and, curiously, with kid gloves, considering its lurid content. *Today's Cinema* (February 12, 1932) called it a "striking adaptation of Robert Louis Stevenson's famous novel ... grips with the realism of its presentation ... affecting love scenes, strong suspense values ... outstanding technical qualities ... Fredric March's work a triumph ... Victorian period admirably suggested ... an entertainment level that will be discussed and argued about wherever it is shown."

"I'll show you what horror means!" Fredric March in *Dr. Jekyll and Mr. Hyde* (1932).

The only negative note in the review concerned Rouben Mamoulian's direction: He "moved his camera a little too freely." Perhaps the excellence of this production, its sterling literary background, plus *Frankenstein*'s acting as a censorial magnet, spared *Dr. Jekyll and Mr. Hyde* a similar fate—at least for a while.

Murders in the Rue Morgue was trade shown on April 14, 1932, at the Prince Edward. The press was anticipating a hit but, oddly, no thought was given to potential censorship problems. Robert Florey was likened to Rene Clair (both being French and former journalists), and a fuss was made over his re-creation of Napoleonic Paris.

Today's Cinema (April 14, 1932) gushed "RUSH FOR *RUE MORGUE*—Edgar Allan Poe Masterpiece" in its headline heralding the trade show, which was sold out. The term "eerie film" was now part of the trade jargon, and *Murders* was, naturally, grouped with *Dracula* and *Frankenstein* in the exhibitors' consciousness, although "with new thrills and new horrors." The trades, somehow, were remaining oblivious to those implications.

The trade show was a success, as the press raved over *Murders'* "brilliant technical qualities" and predicted that the movie would "challenge *Frankenstein*'s records." *Today's Cinema* (April 16, 1932) judged the picture "superior in many respects" to *Frankenstein*, "in sustaining interest and convincing treatment." The SRO audience was described as "appreciative."

Incredibly, the trades urged exhibitors to seize the film, despite unprecedented abuse being heaped upon *Frankenstein*. "Very free and greatly elaborated version of Edgar Allan Poe story," quoth *Today's Cinema*. "The morbidity of the tale has been carefully balanced with charming romantic scenes ... the atmosphere of creeping evil and terrifying detail will have a marked effect. Bela Lugosi plays the part of Dr. Mirakle in a most realistic fashion."

Again, no mention was made of the implied mating of woman and ape or of the crucified prostitute—both the press and censors were, presumably, being kept busy by *Frankenstein*.

Today's Cinema (June 15, 1932) continued singing the praises of *Murders in the Rue Morgue*: "HATS OFF TO LUGOSI" shouted the headline. "UNIVERSAL DOES IT AGAIN—Business Better than *Frankenstein*!" The picture had been cleaning up in the United States and gathering some decent reviews: "Here is a great actor who can coin new thrills." *Washington Post*; "Universal, the movie firm of a thousand shocks, has done it again!" (*Albany Evening News*); "A horrifying and nerve-shattering motion picture" (*Philadelphia Daily News*); and "As thrillers go, it deserves high rating" (*Washington News*). Anticipation was building in the UK for *Murders in the Rue Morgue*'s August 15 release. "It is confidentially anticipated that the same progress will be repeated on this side."

And then, an odd thing happened. Universal, "the movie firm of a thousand shocks," underwent an image change in Britain. *Today's Cinema* (July 4, 1932) announced, "The horror film is out, but in the new season, Universal will introduce the "eerie" picture—*The Old Dark House*, *The Invisible Man*, and *Cagliostro*." Across the Atlantic, Carl Laemmle seemed to be getting the message that all-out horrors like *Frankenstein* would not be welcome in the UK. Just how important was the British market to Hollywood? Were the bans and protests involving *Frankenstein* (and others to follow) enough to persuade Universal (and others) to tone down the horrors or to discontinue their production all together? The introduction of the new Hollywood Production Code in 1934 also contributed to the mix.

Later that week, the Kent County Council suggested an addition to the rating system: films could be classified as "A," "U," or "F" for family. As with other proposed "third certificates," this idea went nowhere.

In the midst of horror movie bashing and the introduction of the "eerie" film, an unidentified minister (*Today's Cinema*, July 10, 1932), actually praised *Frankenstein* from the pulpit. "In contrast with attacks made on *Frankenstein* by fanatical elements in England in the name of religion, I make no apology for bringing this film into the church. It is a gruesome picture but its horrors have a moral and religious significance."

The Old Dark House, the first of Universal's "eerie" pictures, was announced in the British trades in early August. The film's British participants were raved about, as *The Kinematograph Weekly* (August 3, 1921) headlined, "Universal goes British—a marvelously exceptional picture with big box office potential—should be sensational!"

Four days later, Lady Astor addressed Parliament, speaking out against the British Board of Film Censors. "We in the House of Commons," she said (*Today's Cinema*, August 8), "are not at all satisfied about some films. For the trade to appoint their own censor is ridiculous. The government should have the same control over films as they have over the BBC." Mr. R.G. Burnett, author of *The Devil's Camera*—a distinctly anti-movie-tract—went several steps further, claiming that the industry should only make films dealing with Bible history and Christianity. Meanwhile, *Frankenstein* continued to break records across the UK.

"Not a horror movie!" claimed Universal.

Gloria Stuart, Lillian Bond, Charles Laughton, Raymond Massey, Melvyn Douglas, Boris Karloff and Eva Moore in *The Old Dark House* (1932).

That same day, a new "busybody" organization (*Today's Cinema*) launched a new attack on children attending "A" films. The Association of Representative Managers whined that, "scenes and problems exhibited in some films to which children at present have access to are riveted into the subconscious and remain latent for years." While this is probably true, it is also true of real life scenes and problems.

Murders in the Rue Morgue went into general release on September 5, moved back (for unspecified reasons) from its originally announced date of August 15. The picture had "done excellent business in prerelease" (*The Kinematograph Weekly*, August 24, 1932), and so far, had attracted no unwanted interest from either censors or local watch groups.

A trade show was held for the "eerie" *The Old Dark House* at the Picadilly on September 1, 1932. "Gasping Surprises!" shouted the ads. "Trembling Thrills—Thrills—Thrills!" James Whale's followup to *Frankenstein* had all the quirks one would come to expect from this director, and its humor was effectively balanced against its horrors. It seems that Universal was toning down its product, as witnessed by *The Mummy* and especially *The Invisible Man*, which generated as many giggles as gasps.

Today's Cinema (September 1, 1932) headlined *The Old Dark House* as "The First of Eerie Hair Raisers—NO MORE HORROR—Hollywood's New Entertainment Vogue—The 'Eerie' Picture." It was described as a forerunner of several such movies, "definitely *not* in the horror class, like *Frankenstein* or *Dracula*, with at least three scheduled. Unlike *Frankenstein*, thrills will be interspersed with comedy." *Variety* (March 15, 1932) had first noted this trend. "Stories previously placed in the horror class by Universal were now being defined as 'weird mysteries' by this studio, which for a while was wild about horror yarns." A bit of flag waving also crept into the mix: "A triumph of British talent. Fine acting by a distinguished class, intriguing atmosphere, close attention to detail—it reflects the very greatest credit upon all those concerned."

The same day, an announcement was made by the entertainments committee of the Essex County Council, the newest "busybody" organization. "The film industry is of the utmost importance to the future of our nation. It appeals to every class. We want films which tend to uplift the people of our country, young and old." Unfortunately, *Dr. Jekyll and Mr. Hyde* fell short of this lofty vision.

With September 19 set as the release date, the Beckenham Council leaped into action on September 6, banning children from *Dr. Jekyll and Mr. Hyde*, "even if the BBFC does not," and insisting that all local advertising proclaim "not suitable for children."

Further "OBJECTIONS TO DR. JEKYLL" were headlined by the *Kinematograph Weekly* (September 9) as other local watch groups fell in behind Beckenham. Typically, the picture was shown without restrictions in both Croydon and in Bromley, while nearby communities issued bans. On October 11, an attempt made in Belfast by religious groups to ban *Dr. Jekyll and Mr. Hyde* outright was overruled, as the film avoided the onslaught of abuse endured by *Frankenstein*.

Not all of the early horrors raised eyebrows, blood pressure, or howls of protests on the level of *Frankenstein* or *Dr. Jekyll and Mr. Hyde*, yet they still contained the odd scene or concept that, cumulatively, helped to sink the genre.

The Old Dark House was 71 minutes of threats, stylishly served, that were seldom carried through. James Whale brought the picture close to what may have been the pre–Code limit in an exchange between Margaret Waverton (Gloria Stuart), stranded in the titular building, and

Rebecca Femm (Eva Moore). She fondles Margaret's somewhat reveal-ing dinner dress, cackling, "That's finer stuff still, but it'll rot too, in time." *Variety* (November 1, 1932) was not paying much attention, stat-ing that "*Dracula*'s Karloff" was top billed. *Film Weekly* (October 21) was provisionally supportive of the movie, if not its genre. "The vexed ques-tion of the horror film again rears its ugly head (and rears is the word). … Whale and Karloff have progressed since the day when they dabbled in the crude though diverting sensations of *Frankenstein*. There is a new and welcome restraint about their work."

Both *Svengali* (1931) and *White Zombie* (1932) featured hypnotically perverse villains (well played by John Barrymore and Bela Lugosi) who use their powers to sexually dominate the heroines (Marian Marsh, Madge Bellamy). Maestro Svengali places Trilby, a singer young enough to be his granddaughter, in a trance, then has sex with her. "I do love you," she coos, but he is repulsed by his own creation. "You are beautiful, my manufactured love," he says mournfully, "but it is only Svengali talking to himself." *White Zombie*'s Murder Legendre places Madeline into a zombie state to satisfy the lust for a rejected suitor, then desires her for himself. *Variety* (August 2, 1932) was appalled: "revulsion of the more timid against the horrible."

This is pretty strong stuff, even for the pre–Code days, and one pre-sumes that it was *only* in a horror-fantasy context that these perverted sexual dominations could have been permitted. It is odd that *Bride of Frankenstein*, three years later, would spawn unwarranted charges of necrophilia (the monster caresses the face of a female corpse), while Svengali and Legendre were more or less involved in the "real thing." When *White Zombie* was trade shown in London on September 20, 1932, it was merely described as "unblushingly bizarre, lavishly dressed up in a gruesome garb of the macabre" (*Today's Cinema*, September 22).

An odd proposal appeared in the trades in early October: a plan to have one censor for all art forms within the UK. The "A" certificate was under fire yet again, with an excellent point being made. "An 'A' certificate film is still unfit for a child even when he or she is sandwiched between two parents—the effect on the mind is still the same" (*Kinematograph Weekly*, October 2, 1932).

The minds of children were, presumably, not damaged by *The Hounds of Zaroff* (U.S. Title—*The Most Dangerous Game*) when it opened in London two weeks later. *Today's Cinema* (October 22) was put off by the thriller's "blood-thirsty incident and lurid development." High on the lurid scale was a line delivered by Leslie Banks as the mad human-hunter:

Bela Lugosi as Zombie-Master Legendre in *White Zombie* (1932), one of the actor's best horror performances.

Dr. Fu Manchu (Boris Karloff), the "hideous yellow monster" of *The Mask of Fu Manchu* (1932).

"Kill, then love. When you have known that, you will have known ecstasy." A close second must have been a severed head in a jar, or those mounted, like trophies, on Zaroff's wall.

The censorship questions in the UK reached what must have been its nadir in early November of 1932. George McMullen, a Northern Ireland censor, claimed to never have actually *seen* a film, yet he wanted all cinemas banned! That might have seemed to be a good idea to all those of Chinese descent when MGM unleashed *The Mask of Fu Manchu.*

No one knows for sure how MGM, Hollywood's most prestigious studio, came to make two of the era's most vilified horror movies in the same year. After the failure of *Freaks*, one would think that its producer would avoid horror pictures at all costs, but a month after its American release, MGM began production of *The Mask of Fu Manchu.*

Sax Rohmer began his 45 year series of novels with *The Insidious Dr. Fu Manchu* in 1913, and film versions began a decade later with a British serial. Swedish Oriental specialist Warner Oland played the lead in Paramount's *The Mysterious Dr. Fu Manchu* (1929) as something of a wimp—a mistake MGM would soon rectify. Rohmer's latest installment, *The Mask of Fu Manchu*, was scheduled to be published just as the film was to be released—a marketing plan perfect for both Doubleday-Doran and MGM. Despite the bashing taken by *Freaks*, the studio apparently wanted another on-the-edge picture. Backed by the popularity of the character and of Boris Karloff, how could MGM lose?

Motivated by Universal's dual successes with *Dracula* and *Frankenstein*, MGM seemed bent upon duplicating it. While *The Mask of Fu Manchu* was in preparation, MGM began production on *Kongo*, a remake of the 1928: Lon Chaney shocker, *West of Zanzibar*. Starring Walter Huston, this sleazy melodrama practically defined bad taste as the "hero," to avenge himself on the man who paralyzed him, turns his enemy's virginal daughter into an alcoholic hooker. Ironically, she turns out to be *his* daughter.

With *Freaks* and *Kongo* as its predecessors, it is no wonder that *The Mask of Fu Manchu* did not invite close scrutiny from MGM executives. For, in addition to the sexual deviation, drug usage, torture and other niceties that were now commonplace in horror movies, *The Mask of Fu Manchu* added a new wrinkle—racism.

By possessing the mask and sword of Genghis Khan, the evil Dr. Fu Manchu (Boris Karloff) hopes to rally the hordes of Asia to destroy the white race and install himself as ruler of the world. Competing against the "yellow devil" for the relics is a team from the British Museum led

Von Berg (Jean Hersholt) about to get the point in one of many objectional moments in *Mask of Fu Manchu* **(1932).**

by Professor Van Berg (Jean Hersholt) and Scotland Yard's Nayland Smith (Lewis Stone). The expedition locates the treasure but is, in turn, captured by Fu Manchu. Terry Granville (Charles Starrett), Sheila Barton's (Karen Morely) lover, becomes the property of Fu Manchu's perverted daughter Fah So Lee (Myrna Loy), who attempts to drain his will—and more—with her "charms." Smith and Van Berg are also tortured, but all escape in time to destroy Fu Manchu and his dangerous relics before his mad dream is realized.

Cataloging this picture's lapses of taste could take forever, but they can be placed in two groups—racial and sexual. "A Chinaman beat me?" asks an incredulous Van Berg. "Do you suppose for a moment Fu Manchu doesn't know we have a beautiful white girl here with us?" asks an outraged Nayland Smith. "You accursed son of a white dog!" Fu Manchu answers in his own inimitable manner.

Fu Manchu, ever the doting father, has an ingenious method to illicit information from Sir Lionel, a member of the British team:

"Explain to this gentleman the rewards that might be his. Point out to him the delights of our lovely country—the promise of our beautiful women. Even my daughter!" Fu exults. "Even that for you!" Fah Lo See is one of the pre– (or post–) Code's most perverted characters, described even by Myrna Loy as a "sadistic nymphomaniac." Her interest in Terry's whipping—while he hangs half naked from the ceiling—is less than clinical and she can not wait to get her hands on him. "He is not entirely unhandsome is he, my father?" Her loving dad answered, "For a white man, no."

When the MGM brass got a look at what was in the can by mid–August, director Charles Vidor was fired and replaced by Charles Brabin. Greg Mank (*Hollywood Cauldron*) reported that Brabin was removed from *Rasputin and the Empress* by Louis B. Mayer—that film was having problems of its own. Most of what Vidor had shot was re-done, incredibly resulting in what has been previously described. One can only marvel at what the *first* version of *The Mask of Fu Manchu* must have resembled.

The production restarted on September 3, and continued, apparently, along the same path of sex perversion, atrocities and racism as it had under Vidor's control. MGM was, at least, not guilty of hiding what it had wrought. The advertising posters screamed, "Mad, Oriental tortures! Crazed, heartless desires! This Oriental monster almost wrecked civilization with his love drug!"

The *New York Times* (December 2, 1932) review was dismissive of both the picture and its genre: "And still the cinema goes busily about its task of terrorizing the children. The latest of the bugaboo symposium arrived yesterday. To accomplish all (his goals), Fu must acquire the Khan's sacred paraphernalia. ... It is Scotland Yard's job to frustrate Fu if it takes all winter—and this new film does manage to create the unhappy impression that it's taking at least that long." Incredibly, the reviewer failed to mention a word about *The Mask of Fu Manchu*'s unsavory insistence on racism and perversion.

The picture was trade shown in London on December 1, and appalled *Today's Cinema* reviewer with its "lurid scenes of torture ... and mental and physical degradation." At least MGM managed to turn, presumably, a profit in Britain to balance its loss of prestige. That would not be the case with *Freaks*, which was banned without fanfare.

In the half-world populated by Count Dracula and Frankenstein's Monster, one early thirties horror stood out as the ultimate in the grotesque. To most audiences, *Freaks* was the ultimate in bad taste ... and *way* across the line.

Murder Legendre, one of Bela Lugosi's most sinister characters, in *White Zombie* (1932).

Myrna Loy (Fah Lo See) and Boris Karloff (Fu Manchu) as a less than perfect daughter/father team in *The Mask of Fu Manchu* **(1932).**

Director Tod Browning began planning *Freaks* as early as 1927 when, coincidentally, Universal's readers were deciding that Bram Stoker's *Dracula* was too strong for the screen. By 1921, MGM head Louis B. Mayer and producer Irving Thalberg were interested in a horror property to go head-to-head with Universal's monsters and decided to give Browning's five-year-old idea a workout. Unfortunately, *Freaks'* impact on the horror cycle—not to mention critics, audiences and censorship advocates— was completely misjudged. *Freaks* became the most notorious picture of its era, vilified in all quarters. In retrospect, how could it have been otherwise?

Hans (Harry Earles) is a midget who, along with other "mistakes of nature," is exploited in a sleazy carnival. He is infatuated with Cleopatra (Olga Baclanova), a "normal sized" trapeze artist. Spurning Frieda (Daisy Earles), a "small person" who loves him, Hans makes a fool of himself over Cleopatra. She is disgusted by him—and all of the carnival "freaks"—but her interest is piqued when she discovers that Hans is wealthy. She plans, with her lover Hercules (Henry Victor) to get his money—at any cost. A grotesque marriage ensues; Cleopatra plans to gradually poison Hans and inherit his estate. At the wedding feast, as the freaks are about to accept her, Cleopatra breaks, shrieking, "Dirty, slimy freaks!" Now targets of the freaks, she and her lover are mutilated— Hercules is emasculated, and Cleopatra transformed into a "living chicken."

No plot summary or even photograph can convey this movie's power to shock or offend. While one is feeling sorry for the exploited freaks in Browning's *story*, sorrow gradually turns to pity for their exploitation in Browning's *movie*—a movie we are watching for our own amusement! *Freaks* is one movie in which the viewers' emotions range from disgust to pity to shame, and it is incredible that MGM, the world's most prestigious studio, had any involvement in the first place. Consider the catalogue of human misfortune presented as entertainment: Johnny Eck, minus body parts below the waist; Violet and Daisy Hilton, Siamese twins; Frances O'Connor, armless; "pinheads," "living torsos," "dwarves," and so on.

"I wondered if I could go through with it," said "normal" Leila Hyams in David Skals' and Elias Savadas' *Dark Carnival*. "My first reaction was a feeling of intense pity." But, according to Hyams, pity was not warranted or wanted. "The freaks were not at all sorry for themselves. ... They might be sorry for the other fellow ... but none of them was sorry for himself." Perhaps, but it is hard not to feel sorry for *someone*.

Freaks was previewed in January 1932, with the results one would anticipate. Almost half an hour was quickly removed before the picture's February release. It would have been difficult to find a segment of society that was not ready to rail against *Freaks* and, by implication, the industry that spawned it.

The Fox Criterion in Los Angeles was the unlucky recipient of *Freaks'* premiere engagement; it died, as it would later in many metropolitan areas. When the picture played in Washington, D.C., the National Association of Women joined the fray. Mrs. Ambrose N. Diehl, who chaired the group's committee on movies, complained to Will Hays. MGM, panicking, resorted to the same excuse for excess that would appear in the seventies concerning movie violence ("This film stands *against* violence and makes its point by showing the horrors of real violence in as gory a fashion as possible.") The studio tried to present *Freaks* as a human interest drama, concerned with and about the plight of those less fortunate. Most reviewers did not buy it, and called the picture "horrible," "grotesque," "pitiful," "cruel," "bizarre" and "demoralizing."

With great trepidation, MGM released *Freaks* in New York in July, but only after the New York State censor clipped out Cleopatra poisoning Hans' drink, a relatively innocuous scene. The *New York Times* (July 9, 1932) called it "a picture not easily forgotten. The only thing that can be said definitely of *Freaks* is that it is not for children. Bad dreams lie that way."

Freaks performed so badly in New York that MGM ended its run. All told, *Freaks* lost $164,000 (*Dark Carnival*), a huge figure for 1932. Even worse, the picture could not even begin to recoup its losses in the United Kingdom—it was unconditionally banned.

The British finally got to see *Freaks* in 1963, and its delayed release was treated as an event. The cinema press was then far more receptive than the censors had been 31 years earlier, and *Freaks* received good notices, albeit three decades too late to do MGM, Tod Browning, or horror movies much good. A sampling follows:

"I went in quaking. And yet, it doesn't—in retrospect, or even at the time—inspire revulsion. On the contrary, it does what the cinema might do more often—it enlarges one's sympathy by treating something unknown to most of us with compassion and even tenderness. Of course, it is a shock ... but after the first five minutes, when they stop being 'things' and start being people, you start to take them as individuals" (Isabel Quigly).

"Ostensibly a horror film, *Freaks* is in fact a moral allegory. As an attack on complacency, and on the idea of a superior race, *Freaks* is

Two of Tod Browning's *Freaks* (1932), banned in Britain.

uncommonly forceful, one can only wish it had been shown in Nazi Germany" (Eric Rhode).

"Tod Browning's *Freaks* was made in 1932 and was banned ever since. But I've no hesitation in recommending it as a recent work; in some ways it's the most contemporary film on view" (*The Listener*, June 7, 1963).

"Only the most purient and hypersensitive will stint applause for the censor's decision, for *Freaks* remains a film of great honour and humanity. What really happens in the film is that a master of horror uses all his art to combat conventional reactions of horror and revulsion. It is a unique and admirable film" (*Financial Times*, June 14, 1963).

"Browning manages to evoke the closed world of freaks, the intensely human emotions contained in inhuman exteriors, in such a way that fascinated revulsion turns into tender comprehension" (*Sight and Sound*, summer 1963).

These reviews managed to construct a new image for *Freaks*, one that has pretty much been held ever since.

Although H.G.Wells made his early reputation through science fiction classics like *The Time Machine* (1895) and *The Invisible Man* (1897), he intended these romances to be interpreted on more than their surface level. *The Island of Dr. Moreau* (1896) was no exception. Described by Wells biographer Michael Coren as the writer's "most terrifying and successful book," *Dr. Moreau* was a huge hit with both readers and critics. Unfortunately for Wells, this was not enough; he felt that his attacks on creation doctrine and small-minded anti-science protesters were overlooked in favor of the novel's gory excitements. Forty years later, the watchdogs of British sensibility would ban the film version due to its revels in vivisection and bestiality, but there were no such concerns among the staid Victorians.

Wells himself was among the leaders in the attacks against *The Island of Lost Souls* (1933); he considered the movie to be a vulgarization of his more high-minded literary work. Wells was especially repulsed by the proposed (but not consummated) sexual encounter between man and animal thrown in by Philip Wylie and Waldemar Young.

Paramount was apparently interested in going head-to-head with Universal's horrors and chose to follow its acclaimed *Dr. Jekyll and Mr. Hyde* (1932) with another literary adaptation, this time by an author who, unfortunately, was still around to complain.

Edward Parker (Richard Arlen) is on his way to marry Ruth Thomas (Leila Hyams) when he is shipwrecked. He's picked up by the *SS Covena* but, after a fight with the captain (Stanley Fields), is dropped off, along

Edward Parker (Richard Arlen) and Ruth Thomas (Leila Hyams) don't think much of Dr. Moreau (Charles Laughton) in *Island of Lost Souls* (1933). Neither did the BBFC (*photo courtesy of Randy Vest*).

with Montgomery (Arthur Hohl) and his menagerie, on the island of Dr. Moreau (Charles Laughton). Moreau, a disgraced vivisectionist, has been creating semi-humans from animals through radical surgery in the "House of Pain." Among his creations are M'ling (Tetsu Komai), made from a dog; "The Sayer of the Law" (Bela Lugosi), made from a wolf; and Lota (Kathleen Burke), the Panther Woman. Lota is Moreau's most perfect creation, but he wonders, "Has she a woman's impulses?" He attempts to arouse Parker's interest in her: "He is already attracted ... time and monotony will do the rest." But Lota is still part animal, and Parker rebels. Ruth traces Parker to the island and nearly becomes another of Moreau's "experiments" when she attracts Ouran, a monstrous "maninamal." Montgomery turns against Moreau, who then orders Ouran to murder Ruth's ship captain (Paul Hurst)—in violation of the law against spilling blood. The Sayer confronts Ouran, who reveals Moreau's involvement. The monsters attack Moreau in the "House of

Charles Laughton as Dr. Moreau with Kathleen Burke as Lota, his most successful creation, in *Island of Lost Souls* **(1933). The BBFC banned the picture; it was not shown legally in the UK until the sixties (***courtesy of Randy Vest***).**

Pain"—he has made a mockery of their attempts to be human. Parker, Ruth, and Captain Donohue escape as Lota sacrifices her life to save them.

The Island of Lost Souls' cast was headed and dominated by Charles Laughton, who, as Moreau, created the most perverse mad scientist of them all. Eschewing both the manic fervor of Colin Clive and the detached elegance of Peter Cushing, Laughton appears to have just crawled out from under a very wet rock. His Moreau is truly perverse, and it is more than hinted that he is involved in all *kinds* of nastiness. His interest in mating Parker with the Panther Woman is sickeningly salacious, and it is a wonder that this obscenity got past *any* board of censors.

"I wanted to prove how completely she was a woman," Moreau prissily tells Parker. "Whether she was capable of loving, mating, and having children. She was afraid of Montgomery and myself. Then, you came. Well, she was very much attracted to you. You can see, of course, the possibilities that presented themselves."

The film is populated with scores of grotesque, yet impersonal monsters—dog men, lion men, pig men, and ape men—led by an unrecognizable Bela Lugosi as "The Sayer of the Law." He seems to have been created as much from ham as from wolf, as he mournfully intones the rules by which the creatures must live: "What is the Law? Not to spill blood." Lugosi would find decent roles even more difficult to land after the termination of horror movie production in 1937 indirectly started by this film.

The Island of Lost Souls' most horrifying monster was Lota the Panther Woman, played by an unknown teenager, Kathleen Burke. Slinking through the jungle like a bikini-clad, frizzy-haired hooker, she literally sinks her claws into the unsuspecting hero while Moreau—her pimp—watches with more than scientific curiosity. Even more disturbing than the proposed mating of man and animal is the viewer's disappointment when it does not happen. Burke was discovered as the result of, as Greg Mank reported, "the climax of one of Hollywood's all-time shameless publicity stunts." A nationwide talent search was held with Cecil B. DeMille and Rouben Mamoulian among the "judges." Both the contest and Burke were headline grabbers, as was the controversial movie itself.

Following *The Island of Lost Souls'* American release on January 11, 1933, most reviewers were unimpressed by the film's blatancy. The *New York Times* (January 13) observed: "The attempt to horrify is not accomplished with any marked degree of subtlety"; The *New York Evening Post* (January 13) offered: "The picture strains too much for its horror effects."

British critics never had a chance to attack *The Island of Lost Souls*; by April, 1933, the film was banned in the UK, Sweden, and Denmark. In Australia, an unbelievably "politically incorrect" decision was made— Aborigines were forbidden to see the picture, but those of British descent could.

The film did not get a full UK release until 1958. In July 1975, *The Island of Lost Souls* was shown at London's Electric Cinema Club, and received a fair amount of press coverage. David Robinson (*The London Times*, July 14) wrote, "The Electric Cinema Club is presenting a series of films under the title, 'Censored—and Why' to illustrate some of the many obstacles that face films. Among the films is the 1932 horror film, *The Island of Lost Souls*. H.G. Wells was apparently delighted when [it] was banned, and one can see why: it misses most of the subtler points of his 1896 fable. The film introduces a sexual motive not anticipated in Wells: Moreau seeks to mate his creatures with the young couple who chance upon the island."

In her article "Nasty Notions," Margaret Minxman (*The Daily Mail*, July 12, 1975) wrote, "Censorship, like everything else, is subject to change. It should reflect the attitudes of the society in which it operates. The banned movies of yesterday are accepted today either as objects of division or approval. The Electric Cinema Club brings us the only horror film ever totally banned in Britain. You can understand why the censor found this film too disturbing for mass distribution at the time. Its story about the inevitable mad scientist who turns animals into humans is especially nasty. Even nastier in his notion of mating man and beast."

Although the British may well have been more sensitive about vivisection than in other countries, the movie gave censors far more to worry about. In addition to the appalling idea of sex between animals and humans was the picture's anti–Christian tone. "Mr. Parker," smirks Moreau, "do you know what it means to feel like God?" The consensus of censors seemed to be that *The Island of Lost Souls* violated the teachings of the Bible by Moreau's creation of Lota who, unlike Frankenstein's monster, was apparently human.

Like Dr. Moreau, *The Island of Lost Souls* broke every moral code. It certainly would have violated the Production Code had it been enforced. Created by Will Hays, head of the Motion Picture Producers and Distributors of America in 1930, the Code was "self-regulatory" until Administrator Joseph Breen put his foot down on July 1, 1934.

Several of its tenets were: No film may lower the standards of those who see it or contain sex perversion or any inference to it; pictures shall not infer low forms of sex relationships; and brutality and possible grue-someness be treated within the careful limits of good taste. Obviously, *The Island of Lost Souls* not only broke these standards, it may well have been instrumental in creating their stricter enforcement.

The Island of Lost Souls, with its vivisection, bestiality and mockery of Christian beliefs, should have been a red flag warning that, perhaps, horror movies were going too far in their assault on what the general public would accept. The picture was not a box-office success, certainly in part due to its banning abroad. Since nothing succeeds like success, it seems obvious that the picture helped to end Paramount's brief challenge to the Universal horrors.

"Nevertheless," wrote Bryan Senn ("The Golden Age of Horror," *Midnight Marquee* 45), "*The Island of Lost Souls* dares to be counted among the handful of films that was unafraid to break ground and walk on American cinema taboos. It pulls no punches and makes no apologies."

True enough; but it also may have been instrumental in pulling the rug out from under the fledgling horror genre.

1933-34—Breathing Spell

Nineteen hundred thirty-three dawned quietly as *The Mummy*, one of Universal's "eerie pictures" was announced for a January 11 trade show at London's Prince Edward Cinema. "We have just previewed *The Mummy*," said Universal's S.F. Ditcham, "and I can promise exhibitors that the entire production is one of the most amazing, fascinating, and thrilling pictures ever screened" (*The Cinema*, January 4). "Its appeal is general—by that I mean that the picture will pack any theatre from a West End house to the little cinema in northern Scotland." Universal—if not all of Hollywood—was not anxious to repeat the reception given to *Frankenstein*, *Island of Lost Souls* and *Freaks*, and horror was definitely being soft-pedaled.

Ditcham was only too happy to be able to quote American reviews that made *The Mummy* seem as mainstream as possible: "One humdinger of a thriller, with much more dramatic meat than the average" (*Chicago Tribune*); "It is weird and imaginative and at times beautiful" (*Chicago Daily News*); "*The Mummy* still is not in any sense a horror picture. Only in the startling realism of his makeup does Boris Karloff recall such of his terrifying earlier pictures, say as *Frankenstein*" (*Washington Post*); and, "It has most of the thrills of the 'shock' picture without the gruesomeness of the cycle" (*Hollywood Reporter*).

After the excesses of many 1932 horror movies, *The Mummy* marked a return to the more stately style of *Dracula*, of which it is almost a remake. Im Ho Tep (Boris Karloff), a 3700-year-old Egyptian High Priest, is returned to life through the bumbling of a Renfield-like innocent (Bramwell Fletcher). Calling himself Ardath Bey, the mummy stalks Helen Grosvenor (Zita Johann) who is the reincarnation of his lost love

77

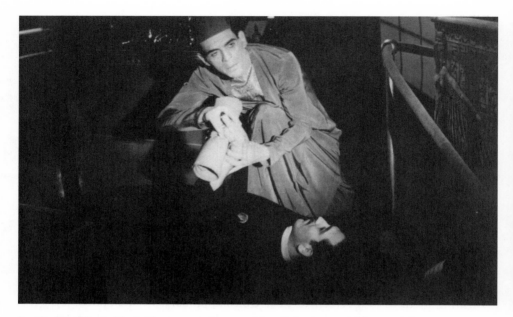

Im Ho Tep (Boris Karloff) recovers the sacred scroll that returned him to life in *The Mummy* (1932).

for whom he died. A battle of wits ensues as Professor Muller (Edward Van Sloan) and Frank Whemple (David Manners) battle Im Ho Tep for Helen's soul. Armed with magical powers, the Mummy nearly succeeds until an ancient goddess intervenes, turning the evil creature into dust.

Although *The Mummy* avoided the visual shocks and sex perversions that typified many early thirties horror movies, its theme of reincarnation may not have played well in Middle America (or Britain). Incredibly, for a film recognized today as a classic, *The Mummy* was completely blown off by *Variety* (January 19, 1933), receiving an innocuous review of 33 lines. By comparison, *Billion Dollar Scandal* (not even mentioned in Leonard Maltin's exhaustive *Movie and Video Guide*) was given 97.

In the UK, *The Mummy* was reverently announced and received ("Fantastic as is its theme, it is offset by the sincerity and conviction of its production"), and was described in *Today's Cinema* (January 13, 1933) as a "reincarnation melodrama" rather than a horror movie. "*The Mummy* scarcely comes under the heading of an action thriller as it is almost completely devoid of the crude mechanics so long inseparable from melodrama. Seems likely to achieve an even greater success than that achieved by previous Karloff films. Karloff's best to date."

Im Ho Tep (Boris Karloff) about to commit an act of blasphemy in *The Mummy* (1932).

A romantic moment between Helen (Zita Johann) and Im Ho Tep (Boris Karloff) in *The Mummy* (1932).

Universal seemed to find the perfect formula with *The Mummy*; horrifying enough for the "addicts," yet so subtly done that not one word was raised against it in the UK. Next to *Frankenstein*, *Murders in the Rue Morgue*, and the banned *Freaks* and *Island of Lost Souls*, *The Mummy* seemed positively harmless.

While *The Mummy* was gaining fans all over the UK, the Home Office was preparing to address the deadly issue of children and "A" films. *Today's Cinema* (January 13) was in favor of this move, feeling that the BBFC lacked the teeth to deal with the problem. Sir Cecil Levita was named chairman, and was described as being "broad minded and liberty loving."

The Mummy premiered at the London Capital on February 5, and the cinema press was enthusiastic in its reporting of the picture's huge American success. Hundreds were turned away at the Capitol as *The Mummy*, "Universal's latest essay into the eerie," drew queues that wrapped around the blocks. Meanwhile, *The Monkey's Paw*—now seemingly lost—was trade shown with a cautionary warning: "Excellent general entertainment with possible exception of squeamish patrons."

Based on W.W. Jacobs' famous tale about being careful what you wish for (a mutilated corpse is wished back from the grave), *Today's Cinema* (February 16, 1933) praised the production for having "the dreads left to the imagination."

On March 7, the Home Office ruled on "Children and 'A' Films" and "Horror Pictures." Citing an earlier (December 16, 1929) ruling, the H.O. decreed that children may attend "A" pictures with an adult, but added that "parents must be given every opportunity to know about the film's content." As for horror, "During the course of the last year, the Committee's attention was drawn to a few unusually horrifying films which, it was represented, were particularly unsuitable for children. After viewing these films, the Committee decided that, although they were passed 'A' by the BBFC, some further action was desirable to ensure that parents were especially warned not to take young children to see them." This action brought the "H" certificate a step closer.

The Kinematograph Weekly (March 9, 1933) opined that, "The fanatics who hold that all children should be excluded from 'A' films have been entirely confounded by these findings. What may be quite unsuitable for a child of tender years may well be the best possible entertainment for a boy or girl of 14 or 15; and actual practical experiment has shown that parents are less unsatisfactory judges of what is good for their children than anyone else."

A week later, *King Kong*, which was having some censorship problems of its own in the United States, was playing simultaneously at both of New York's Radio City theatres, breaking all New York box office records. Local boards in the United States were concerned about Kong's trampling and eating islanders, and this problem would follow the ape across the Atlantic.

Victor Harrison and Charles Crotch, owners of the Plaza Cinema in Norwich, were fined the incredible amount of £1 on March 14 for allowing approximately 400 children to see the "A" certificate *Death Ray*. Harrison claimed he thought the picture was "U," but was found guilty anyway. However, he certainly came out ahead financially.

Two days later, Warner Bros.' Technicolor release *Mystery of the Wax Museum* was trade shown at the Prince Edward, and was described as a "weird masterpiece of mystery" (*Today's Cinema*, March 17). The picture had been described in less glowing terms in America—David J. Skal (*The*

Lionel Atwill as mad sculptor Ivan Igor in *Mystery of the Wax Museum* (1933) in a short that was probably not appreciated by censors (*courtesy of Randy Vest*).

Monster Show) quoted B.O. Skinner, director of the Ohio Department of Film Censorship, in a complaint to Warner Bros.: "We are, as you know, approving this film with eliminations. I wish, however, to register a formal protest against the film. I feel it would be much better for all of us if productions of this type of film would be discontinued." The British were not amused by Lionel Atwill's Technicolored dripping face as mad sculptor Ivan Igor, who covered human corpses with wax after his hands had been destroyed in a fire. Igor showed such an obsessive interest in the female wax figures, it is incredible that the censors either missed or ignored the necrophilic element. (Oddly, the British censors would soon have no trouble recognizing the "necrophillic" aspects of *Bride of Frankenstein*.) The film's climax is one of horror's most memorable: Fay Wray smashes Atwill's wax mask, revealing a facial disfigurement that equaled

an Igor (Lionel Atwill) with two friends in *Mystery of the Wax Museum* (1933) (*courtesy of Randy Vest*).

Lon Chaney's *Phantom of the Opera*. "Nauseating!" cried the British censors, but the public was about to vote with its tickets.

Today's Cinema (March 9, 1933) editorialized on the question of censors and children. "It is distinctly unfair that a working man and his wife, who have a young child, should be precluded from attending a cinema because they are unable to take their child with them."

A trade show was held on March 23, and both the picture and Lionel Atwill came away unscathed. "In its particular field of horror and thrill," said *Today's Cinema* (March 24), "this calculated shocker indeed delivers the goods. It seems entirely safe to say that it has moments of macabre sensation which have not been matched in any film of its type to date. Acting honours are easily earned by Lionel Atwill in his gripping yet appealing study." Although *Mystery of the Wax Museum* was compared to *Frankenstein*, it failed to generate any of the attacks as did the earlier picture. The closest thing to a rap in *Today's Cinema* was this sexist comment: "a mask which falls to pieces under the hand of a girl, revealing a revoltingly scarred and twisted mass of facial horror which will bring even the most hard-boiled woman patron to the edge of her seat."

King Kong, after its New York triumph, conquered London in early April. *The Kinematograph Weekly* (April 12, 1933) called the picture "the most marvelous film ever produced; certainly it is the most brilliant technical achievement in the history of the industry." Few would argue that point, and no mention was made in the British trade press of negative reactions to the giant ape's slaughters.

Horror films in general, though, continued to be kept under close scrutiny. In Portsmouth, the Home Office Circular on films advised all exhibitors to place notices outside their cinemas that the picture playing was not suitable for children. Mr. V. Pannell, a Portsmouth cinema owner, spoke what amounted to a death sentence for horror movies. "If I find a film unsuitable," he said (*The Cinema*, April 19), "I arrange for a change. If other exhibitors exercised the same care with regard to films which were likely to be shown to children, it would prevent the authorities introducing stringent regulations." These "stringent regulations" would become the "H" certificate; either way, the situation was not good for horror.

"If they put on a substitute programme at matinees," countered Mr. F.B. Blake, "adults who come to see the thriller will complain."

As the old questions of children at horror movies continued to be debated, *The Mummy* was shattering records throughout Britain, including house records set by *Frankenstein* and *The Old Dark House*. And,

King Kong (1933), aghast at some censorial snipping.

while *Mystery of the Wax Museum* was beginning its uncertain run in the UK, Lionel Atwill made a second, more disturbing appearance.

Atwill, horror's second-team Karloff/Lugosi, played some pretty sick characters in his career (and, as revealed in his 1940s sex scandal trial, in his life, as well). But, few could approach the pervert he played to perfection in *Murders in the Zoo* (1933). This Paramount production opens with one of the most horrific scenes ever, one that was way over the line even in the pre–Code era.

A man lies on the jungle floor, held down by two natives, while Eric Gorman (Lionel Atwill) laboriously engages in an unseen (by us) activity while bent over the captive. He appears to be sewing something while the man groans and kicks in pain. "A Mongolian prince taught me this, Taylor," Gorman intones. "An ingenious device for the right occasion. You'll never lie to a friend again, and you'll never kiss another man's wife." The man, Taylor, staggers upright and careens into the bush. As he approaches us, we see that his lips, like those on a shrunken head, have been sewn shut.

Gorman returns to camp, and to his wife Evelyn (Kathleen Burke), who asks about the missing Taylor; as if on cue, a native arrives to announce that Taylor has been killed by a tiger. Evelyn confides her suspicions and horror of Gorman to Roger Hewitt (John Lodge), who wants to settle things with her husband and have Gorman, a millionaire and supporter of the Municipal Zoo, arrive in the United States with his latest shipload of animals. He is met by alcoholic newsman Peter Yates (Charlie Ruggles), who has just been hired as the zoo's press agent. Dr. Woodford (Randolph Scott) examines a green mamba, the deadliest snake on earth, as Professor Evans (Harry Beresford) tells Gorman of the zoo's financial problem. Yates and Gorman decide to have a fundraising dinner at the zoo when Hewitt, seated across from Gorman, is killed by the mamba venom. Evelyn finds a severed snake head in their home, its fangs dripping venom, and guesses the truth. Gorman follows her to the zoo and, before she can show the incriminating head to Dr. Woodford, throws her into an alligator-filled pond. Gorman blames Woodford's carelessness for both deaths. His actions cause the zoo to be shut down. Meanwhile, Woodford and Yates have determined that the green mamba could not have killed Hewitt. When Gorman is confronted by Woodford, he stabs the doctor with the snake head, leaving him for dead. He is saved by a just discovered serum as Gorman, now on the run, is chased into a cage by lions where a python constricts him to death.

Although *Murders in the Zoo* attempted to lighten its grim premise with Charlie Ruggles' (unwelcome) "comedy," this is one nasty picture,

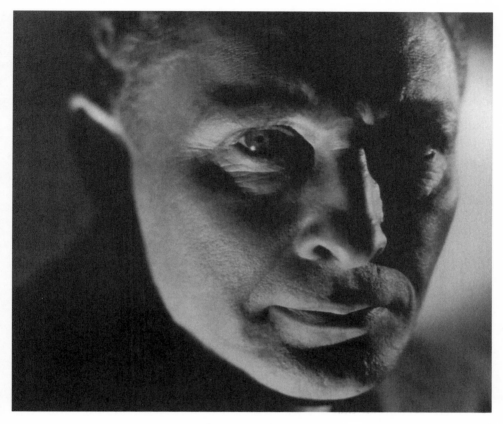

Lionel Atwill as Eric Gorman, perhaps the nastiest villain in thirties horror movies, in *Murders in the Zoo* **(1933)** (*courtesy of John Antosiewicz and Glenn Damato*).

among the most "objectional" of the early horrors. Director Edward Sutherland could not and did not hide behind Gothic fairy tale trappings; the movie is presented in a completely realistic milieu. Eric Gorman is arguably the most loathsome villain in horror history—he has absolutely *no* redeeming characteristics. At least Charles Laughton's Dr. Moreau (another strong candidate) was trying to *prove* something; Gorman is a sadistic, insanely jealous sex pervert, aroused by his wife's loathing of him.

Sex is never far from Gorman's mind as he kills for it and takes it from his terrified wife. In one particularly ugly scene, Gorman literally manhandles the luckless Evelyn and he forces her to kiss him. As they struggle, his hand nearly touches her breast, a shocking scene for 1932.

The picture takes great pains to identify Gorman as being no different from the animals he captures. They may well be the only living things for which he has any respect. "They're honest in their simplicity," he says, "their primitive emotions. They love, they hate, they kill." In this respect, Gorman is similar to Zaroff in RKO's *The Most Dangerous Game* (1932), as they are both aroused by death and brutality. Animals play a major role in another of *Murders in the Zoo*'s scenes of questionable taste — a no-holds-barred battle involving several big cats that is disturbing because it is real.

The London Times' reviewer (June 12, 1933) was unimpressed, stating, "There is little or no mystery about any of these murders and the murderer is a plain, unvarnished villain. This collector of reptiles for a zoological society is singular in nothing except his readiness to take human life. The narrative is plain and workmanlike." The reviewer did not comment on the opening sequence, because apparently it was censored for the UK release. "In the jungle, Gorman's wife is kissed by a member of the expedition," the review continues. "The culprit is *bound and left to the lions.*"

Murders in the Zoo suffered an even worse fate elsewhere; it was banned in several countries, including Australia (and other British Commonwealth nations), Sweden, and even in Nazi Germany. Paramount itself was forced into self-censorship when, in September of 1935, the studio re-released the picture. The offending sequence was altered.

Despite the gruesomeness and general depravity of the film, there is one *very* funny bit not supplied by the spectacularly unfunny "comedy" of Charlie Ruggles. A distraught Mrs. Gorman asks her husband what Taylor said before (as Gorman lied to her) he "left." "He didn't say anything," the psycho answers calmly.

As Bryan Senn pointed out (*Midnight Marquee* 48), "With more emphasis on the infrequent but effective *dark* humor rather than on the sledgehammer-style *light* humor, *Murders in the Zoo* could have joined the ranks of such hard-hitting classics as *Freaks* (1932), *Island of Lost Souls* (1933), and *Mad Love* (1935)." The picture was nasty enough as it was, though, to attract the scrutiny of censors everywhere.

The offensive opening scene appears to have been cut from all of *Murders*' British prints; no mention was made of it following the picture's May 16 trade show for an October 30 release. "It will be seen that the development proceeds on shock lines, but the incident is so well maintained that the onlooker will be more conscious of entertainment than of repulsion at its calculated callousness. Excellent popular

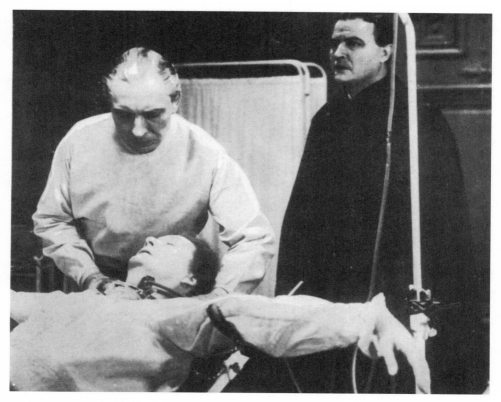

Mad Doctor von Niemann (Lionel Atwill) up to no good in *The Vampire Bat* **(1933).**

entertainment off the beaten track" was the verdict of *Today's Cinema* (May 17, 1933), an opinion not shared by the rest of the world of the film in its complete version.

Atwill was as plentiful in London that spring as fish and chips: *The Vampire Bat* ("Bidding only for sensation and thrill") was trade shown with *Murders in the Zoo*. This foolishly inoffensive effort cast Atwill as a mad scientist bent on creating life in his lab while the village idiot, Dwight Frye, takes the blame for Atwill-induced murders.

The British finally entered the horror market with Boris Karloff's *The Ghoul*, which was trade shown on July 25. Scheduled for an October 16 release, the picture marked a triumphant return for Karloff, who had not been in his homeland for years. *The Ghoul* had been considered a "lost" film, but it resurfaced in the seventies to general dismay. Despite the picture's historical significance, it is practically unwatchable. *Today's*

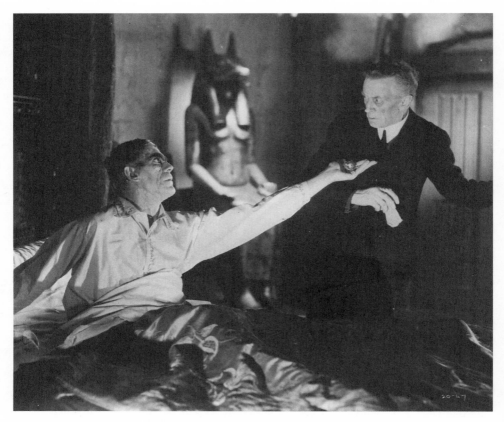

Boris Karloff as *The Ghoul* (1933), startling Ernest Thesiger as Laing (*courtesy of Randy Vest*).

Cinema (July 25), however, was enthusiastic: "*The Ghoul* strikes a new note in macabre melodrama in that it possesses a more feasible explanation than is usual and is developed with an extraordinary attention to detail."

Murders in the Zoo, even in its short form, attracted the attention of the Home Office due to the scene involving fighting felines. On July 28, 1933, David Grenfell, member of Parliament, questioned the desirability of exhibiting pictures in which wild animals were forced to fight on camera. That same day, the BBFC attempted to explain its confusing stance on horror movies. "It has been argued," said Sir Cecil Levita (*Today's Cinema*), "that if a film is suitable for adults, it is consequently unsuitable for children. The Board does not say that. We don't say because the film is 'A' that it is necessarily harmful for children. We *are* one and all agreed that a film that frightens a child is something a child should not see—horrific films should not be shown to children."

On August 15, the Home Secretary looked back on the previous meeting while attending the Home Office Consultative Committee on Censorship: "The last meeting held was to discuss with the censors the subject of 'horrific' films. Other meetings will be held from time to time" (*Kinematograph Weekly*). He added cryptically, "In case of any real problem, the machinery is there to handle it." As of mid–August, the BBFC had only listed *one* picture released in 1933 as "horrific." *The Cinema* declined to identify the movie.

Horror movies were not the only pictures under censorial scrutiny that summer—incredibly, *The Sign of the Cross* was banned in Bristol. Three other localities also planned to ban the picture, but withdrew the ban after consulting with the BBFC. About 300 feet of the film were considered to be "unsuitable," but the BBFC felt that "no reasonable person could take exception" (*Kinematograph Weekly*, August 17, 1933).

Two days later, *King Kong* attracted some unwanted attention from Midland watch groups. Representatives from Warwick, Wolverhampton, and Sutton Coldfield trooped to the Birmingham Forum for a private showing. To be decided was whether special conditions needed to be placed on *King Kong* for public showings. This controversial move added to the ludicrous situation regarding *Frankenstein* being banned in one area and playing in an adjacent one. Meanwhile, *King Kong* continued to break records throughout the UK, with thousands being turned away in Cardiff and Glasgow.

Liverpool, a hotbed of contradictory attitudes towards "A" films, returned, on October 18, to its position of banning children from them unilaterally. Middlesex took an opposing position a week later. "It has been suggested that children should be entirely excluded where 'A' films are being shown," said a spokesman for the county council (*Today's Cinema*, October 26). "But the committee does not favour this as these films are not necessarily harmful to every child. The BBFC sometimes pass for exhibition films which might have a horrifying effect upon audiences. Although these films had been passed with an 'A' certificate, further action was desirable to ensure that parents were specially warned."

Universal's next foray into the "eerie," *The Invisible Man*, was announced in the trades as a sensation. "One of the secrets in the industry is about to be solved," (*The Cinema*, November 18, 1933), "for *The Invisible Man* has now been shipped from New York to London. The secret of *The Invisible Man* is still a secret, except to a handful of

Prof. Morlant (Boris Karloff) on the prowl in *The Ghoul* **(1933), Britain's first entry in the "horrific" sweepstakes (***courtesy of Randy Vest***).**

technicians, the cast, and one or two New York executives. The picture was made behind closed doors. As in *The Old Dark House*, this latest James Whale vehicle is almost entirely British."

The Invisible Man premiered at San Diego's Spreckles Theatre, and S.F. Ditcham, Universal's man in London, reported that the opening day's take was gigantic and moving towards record-breaking status. British exhibitors were holding their breaths in anticipation, after the picture replaced *King Kong* both at New York's Roxy and as the "screen's most remarkable achievement." *The New York American* called the picture "one of the best yet produced"; The *New York Times* felt the film to be "superb cinematic material"; *The Daily Mirror* enthused, "a stupendous thriller, remarkable, and magnificent"; and *The New York Daily News* said, "both comic and scary—heartily recommended."

With press like this, it is clear why *The Invisible Man*'s November 30 London trade show was eagerly anticipated. Curiosity at just *how*

Despite *The Invisible Man*'s (1933) comical moments, Griffin (Claude Rains) had his nasty side.

Claude Rains' invisibility would be presented attracted the British just as it had American audiences. The picture's surprising reliance on comedy, though, was not a staple of H.G. Wells' novel. "Mad scientist" Jack Griffin (Claude Rains) has discovered that "monocaine," a rare drug, can bleach the body into invisibility. What he discovers too late is that it also drives a person mad. After terrorizing a hotel run by Mrs. Hall (Una O'Connor), he finds a reluctant ally in Kemp (William Harrigan), who soon turns traitorous. When Griffin avenges himself against Kemp, though, the *Invisible Man*—both character and movie—turns downright nasty. Griffin binds Kemp to his car and plans to push both over a cliff. "You'll run gently down and through the railings," Griffin gloats. "Then you'll do a somersault and probably break your arms. Then a grand finish-up with a broken neck. Well, goodbye Kemp. I always said you were a dirty little coward. You're a dirty, stinking little rat as well."

This did not go unnoticed by *Today's Cinema* (December 2), whose reviewer mentioned the picture's odd conceit of alternating "cold-blooded murder with broad comedy. Hearty laughter greeted quite a number of what were really blood-chilling incidents." The climax was described as "gruesome."

Perhaps in partial response to negative criticism garnered by his horrors, Universal president Carl Laemmle issued this statement to the British trades (July 4, 1934): "I will not make dirty pictures. I am for decent pictures." Laemmle characterized himself as a "family man," which must have been funny to industry insiders; Laemmle was infamous for his nepotism.

The year started quietly—no pictures were released in Britain that were overly horrific, the *Frankenstein* furor was long dead, and not much was being made of *Murders in the Zoo*, probably the most objectional horror of 1933. There was time for reflection, and *Today's Cinema* (July 11, 1933) was doing plenty of it. In an editorial titled "Our Critics—and Their Friendly Cooperation," the following points were made:

1. Everyone of us has different likes, dislikes, and ideals.

2. Even if a person or event could be regarded as perfect from one point of view, there is still the question of taste to be considered.

3. It has always been the desire of this industry to accomplish an almost impossible task—to please everybody.

4. Our business is essentially a family business, and parents are notoriously critical of the entertainments to which they take their children. On the other hand, it cannot be expected that an entertainment which draws its revenue from the adult should bring its entertainment down entirely to the level of the juvenile.

5. It is curious that a Western invariably gets a "U" certificate—while murder is confined to an "A." Murders only appear to earn a "U" when they are carried out by cowboys.

This grousing was instigated by the formation of the Legion of Decency by the Catholic Church in America. The British industry was being inundated by what the trades called "busybody" critics, and apparently feared more of the same from the other side.

The brief respite ended when Universal's *The Black Cat* was trade shown in London on July 28. Retitled *The House of Doom*, the picture was among the most offensive—on either side of the Atlantic—of all the early horrors.

The Black Cat (1934) was the first, best, and inevitable teaming of KARLOFF (as he was billed) and Bela Lugosi, then the world's ranking horror stars. The pair would appear together eight times, including their walk-ons in *Gift of Gab* (1934), until their basically one-sided partnership ended with Karloff's greatest performance as *The Body Snatcher* (1945). Karloff always received the better billing and salary, and except for *Son of Frankenstein* (1939), usually gave the better performance. In *The Black Cat*, though, the two were fairly evenly matched.

Honeymooners Peter (David Manners) and Joan Allison (Jacqueline Wells) meet Dr. Vitus Werdegast (Bela Lugosi) as the trio travel to Budapest. Werdegast is on his way to meet with an "old friend," architect Hjalmar Poelzig (Boris Karloff), for whom he bears a mysterious grudge. Joan is injured in an accident and is taken to Poelzig's futuristic house. Poelzig, now the leader of a Satanic cult, had deserted his post during the war, leaving Werdegast to rot in a POW camp for 15 years. In the meantime, he stole his "friend's" wife, murdered her, and married their daughter Karen (Lucille Lund). He displays his first "wife," along with the corpses of other female victims, like trophies, in an underground chamber. Complicating matters are Werdegast's pathological fear of cats and his interest in Joan, an interest shared by Poelzig. When Joan recovers, she meets Karen and, discovering her identity, informs her that Werdegast (whom she thought to be dead) is very much alive. Poelzig, after eavesdropping, kills Karen, whom he previously described as "the very core of my being." He selects Joan for the cult's sacrificial virgin, but Werdegast rescues her. After discovering Karen's corpse, he goes mad and, after chaining Poelzig to a torture rack, flays him alive. The ineffectual Peter finally takes action but, mistaking Werdegast's actions, foolishly shoots him. Dying, Werdegast pulls a lever that dynamites the castle.

Edgar Allan Poe, like Karloff and Lugosi, was a top horror star— perhaps the first—and teaming the trio seemed like a natural. Unfortunately, there is little in Poe's writing that is cinematic (as his adaptors soon found out) and nothing of his original story in this picture. Poe's tale, written in 1843, concerned an initially kind, animal-loving husband and his downfall due to drink. His degradation begins with his abuse of his pets; he finally mutilates and kills Pluto, a black cat. He turns his wrath upon his wife, and walls her up in the basement. His crimes are revealed by a second, mysterious cat resembling Pluto.

Bela Lugosi (as Dr. Werdegast), despite appearances, is the hero (more or less) in *The Black Cat* (1934), shown here with Jacqueline Wells as Joan.

The satanic Poelzig (Boris Karloff) in *The Black Cat* (1934).

This unfilmable plot was completely jettisoned by Universal; Peter Ruric's script was a wallow on the wild side. Michael and John Brunas and Tom Weaver described the picture (in *Universal Horrors*) as "a veritable catalogue of human corruption. Sadism, shades of incest, revenge, murder, torture, voyeurism, Satan worship, ailurophobia, necrophilia, and insanity are weaved into the nearly plotless story with remarkable precision."

Somehow, director Edgar G. Ulmer managed to whip this mess together into an elegant, although distasteful, feast for those so inclined to dine. Even though *The Black Cat* was surrounded by more than its share of perverse horror (and non-horror) movies in these pre–Code days, it still managed to stand out from the pack. Ruric's script, which contained far more repellent images than reached the screen, was completed on February 19, 1934. The filming began on the 28th. Scheduled for a lightning-fast 15 days, the movie was, incredibly, in release on May 7, beating the new code by three months. How this exercise in perversion—code or no code—ever got past the censor is not certain.

Greg Mank (*Karloff and Lugosi*) reported that Carl Laemmle, Universal president, was vacationing in Germany when the script was completed. Carl Jr., the nominal producer, was in a New York courtroom in mid–February and was, apparently, oblivious to the whole thing. When *someone* in charge finally saw the finished print, though, all hell broke loose.

Laemmle, Sr., ordered revisions, which were shot between March 25 and 28. One can only wonder about the effect *The Black Cat* produced in its original form, since the re-shot version is sick enough as it is. Unfortunately, in addition to toning things down, the revisions left the "plot" incomprehensible.

A glance at the original script, dated February 27, 1934, reveals just what Ruric and Ulmer were really up to. The two protagonists seem to have had a much greater sexual interest in Joan, as indicated in Sequence F, shots 8 to 11: "Joan is in silhouette in immediate foreground. (Werdegast) is looking at her with a little more than paternal expression. Poelzig might well be contemplating a very delectable piece of French pastry. Werdegast's expression leaves even less to the imagination." What was actually shot is Poelzig fondling—then gripping—a statue of a reclining nude in the foreground as Peter and Joan embrace in the background.

Shot F-44 has the "kindly" Dr. Werdegast shooting up Peter with a drug. "Werdegast takes the narcotic case from his pocket, and rolls up Peter's sleeve." As filmed, Peter is knocked down by Werdegast's servant.

Vitus, as originally scripted (Shot G-13), enters Joan's room where she lies unconscious. (A marginal note requests the scene to be "definitely underplayed, if you please, Mr. Lugosi.") As Werdegast approaches Joan, he murmurs, "You are very beautiful." She awakens as he touches her hair. "Have you ever heard of Satanism?" he asks (G-15). "The worship of the Devil...or Evil?" This exchange would cause a furor in the UK, where all references to Satanism were excised and replaced by a "Cult of Sun Worshippers."

The final scene—Poelzig's death by torture—is rough enough as played, but Ruric had an even more lurid idea. "I'm going to tear your putrid, stinking skin from your body," grimaces Werdegast (Shot J-16). "Slowly—a little at a time." Ruric's description of the scene is stomach-turning (Shot J-19). "The wall. The shadow of Werdegast and Poelzig. An effect as if Werdegast was splitting the scalp slowly, pulling the sheath of skin down over Poelzig's head and shoulders. Poelzig, sans skin, is struggling on the rack. By a superhuman effort, he frees himself and falls to the floor. Poelzig raises his hideous body—his eyes focused dully, expressionlessly, on Joan. He laboriously, painfully, crawls toward her."

Naturally, none of this ever actually appeared on a theater screen, but it is incredible that Peter Ruric and Edgar Ulmer thought that it could. *The Black Cat*, even in its sanitized form, made very few friends critically, although audiences loved it; the picture was Universal's top grosser (in more ways than one) for the year.

As it was with *Murders in the Rue Morgue*, The *New York Times* review (May 19, 1934) was more concerned with the film's departure from Poe than with its questionable content: "The acknowledgment which the producer of *The Black Cat* graciously makes to Edgar Allan Poe seems a trifle superfluous since the new film is not remotely to be identified with Poe's short story. A clammy and excessively ghoulish tale of hi-jinks in a Hungarian horror salon, *The Black Cat* is more foolish than horrible. The story and dialogue pile the agony on too thick to give the audience a reasonable scare."

1935—Steps
Must Be Taken

"I think," said filmmaker Basil Dean (*The Daily Cinema*, January 2, 1935), "the best thing that could happen to the industry in 1935 ... would be a return of the Censorship which at present appears to me to be sadly in need of a thorough overhaul. The British censorship of films at present is erratic, willful, unconstitutional, and completely without any intellectual understanding." Very few could argue that point, and, in 1935, the problem—especially involving horror pictures—would grow worse in the UK.

In Ireland, 117 movies had been banned in 1934 out of 2,275 presented. While that is only 5 percent of the total, 117 is still an incredibly large number. It is doubtful that *any* "horrifics" were spared.

The Archbishop of Canterbury consulted with the Prime Minister in early January, heading a group consisting of the National Cinema Inquiry Committee, the National Council of Women, the National Union of Teachers, the Free Church Council, the Salvation Army, and the Public Morality Council. The topic: according to the group, 25 percent of all pictures passed by the censor were unfit for public screening. The Prime Minister was asked to create a commission to investigate their claims.

The Wigan Watch Committee, at the same time, addressed the advisability of showing films *not* passed by the British Board of Film Censors, since it seemed to make little difference to the public if a picture had a BBFC certificate in the first place. It was decided that such a movie should be presented to the Watch Committee six weeks before the planned exhibition so that the committee could have a "private showing" to determine if the film could be screened. This was in open defiance of the BBFC and illustrates the censors' weakness. Unlike the Wigan Committee, the Archbishop's group did not want to reflect poorly on the BBFC, but, addressing the considerable influence that films exert on children, felt that *someone* had to do *something*. The main concerns of the group were, not surprisingly, sex and horrific violence.

The deputation to the Prime Minister did not pass unnoticed by the trades; *Today's Cinema* (January 16, 1935) was outraged. "Who are these independent investigators?" the paper justly asked. "What are their special qualifications for judging the suitability of an entertainment that is patronized every week in Great Britain alone by nearly twenty million people? Is the suggestion that all twenty million cinema goers are fools or patrons of vice?"

An "open letter" to the leaders of the deputation followed two days later. "How many of you precious people go regularly to the cinema?" it asked. "Do the ladies and gentlemen backing your move pay periodic visits to the cinemas, much less see all the films they scarify so trenchantly? If they and you have not, then what right have you to condemn the pictures as bad or to suggest their influence is harmful?"

Nineteen thirty-five was one of screen horror's most prolific years and produced two of the genre's best: *Bride of Frankenstein* and *Mad Love*. The year in the UK got off to a rather slow start with *The Return of Chandu*, which was dismissed by *Today's Cinema* (February 2): "The level of direction, presentation, and acting is no higher than the theme calls for, a fact that is hardly likely to weigh very heavily with the less critical type of patronage for whom it is obviously designed." This Bela Lugosi vehicle raised no eyebrows; neither did, surprisingly, *The Mystery of Edwin Drood*, despite its main character's (Claude Rains) drug addiction. Offense *was* taken by *Today's Cinema* (March 20) against the latest trade of censorship "busybodies." "GET TO ARMS!" shouted a headline. "OUR LIVELIHOOD IS AT STAKE! GRAVE CENSORSHIP DANGER!"

Taking their lead from a perceived "purity drive" in the United States, the British Board of Film Classification began puzzling over the "A" certificate. *The Kinematograph Weekly* (March 28, 1935) announced that too many children under the age of 16 were finding their ways into cinemas and that much stricter enforcement was necessary.

The concern was not just over horrific content, but also sex—horror's all too frequent companion. *The Kinematograph Weekly* (April 4) addressed the problem in economic terms. "Something is wrong in the Film World this minute—seriously wrong. This is no matter of morals, though it has been widely misrepresented as such. The distortion of sex-life and love that we get on the screen probably do little moral harm ... *but they keep the family away*. We are not in film business for our health, but to make money."

The two-headed monster of sex and horror was disrupting the film business on both sides of the Atlantic. Both British and American leaders felt that censorship was no real solution to the problem of declining attendance and mounting criticism. "When we first started our work," said Mrs. James Looram, chairman of the International Federation of Catholic Alumnae (*Kinematograph Weekly*, May 16), "we thought censorship was the solution. Then we discussed our mistake. Educating the quality of public demand while the producers worked with us to improve entertainment to meet this demand has solved the problem." One can only wonder if Mrs. Looram would consider the "problem solved" if she visited any cinema in the United States or Britain today.

Louis B. Mayer, who hosted a meeting on the subject at MGM studios, felt that the recent outcry would be a positive force in filmmaking. "After all," he said, "ours is a business. We have our stockholders to account to. We have to note what the public patronizes." Apparently, Mrs. Looram and Mr. Mayer felt that if the public's taste in films improved (meaning less sex and horror), the film industry would respond in kind, making censorship unnecessary.

In early May of 1935, Will Hays suggested that Martin Quigley, editor of the *Motion Picture Herald* and *Motion Picture Daily*, go to London to explain the American Production Code to the Film Producers Group of the Federation of British Industries. Quigley said (*The Kinematograph Weekly*, May 16), "In view of the fact that certain definite policies governing the subject matter of motion pictures have been adopted in America, the British producer is entitled to be advised specifically of these policies so that the Production Code shall amount to neither hindrance nor handicap to the British producer in his efforts to obtain representation in the American market."

In a telling statement, Quigley mentioned one of the causes of the death-blow to Hollywood horror. "The American industry also is mindful of the enthusiastic reception which always has been accorded to its films in all the English speaking markets outside the United States. That there should be this coincidence is naturally inevitable, because among right-thinking, civilized peoples the world over, there is unanimity upon matters of common decency and morality." Among these "right-minded people," it must be assumed, there is no place for pictures like *The Island of Lost Souls* or *Freaks*.

London in 1935 boasted 258 cinemas with 344,000 seats. These seats were becoming increasingly easier to find vacant as more films were being made that were "unsuitable" for children. Also, it was felt that far too many cinema managers were allowing children to see adult films. The situation had become so bleak that London area schools began teaching their students the difference between "A" and "U" films.

As film producers, cinema managers, and moviegoers waited, the British government continued to do nothing about its proposed entry into censorship. *The Kinematograph Weekly* (May 9, 1935) noted that, "Sir John Gilmour, Home Office Commissioner, is not ready to announce the Government decision on censorship." Although Parliament may not have been ready, many local governments were. Within five months, the Leicester Watch Committee decided to ban *Bride of Frankenstein* for *all* patrons, regardless of their age.

Added to the British sex-and-horror censorship mix was the age-old question of cinemas on Sunday. In our enlightened times (when anyone can do practically anything anytime), it is easy to forget that Sunday was once a true "day of rest." In Margate, a North Sea resort, the Watch Committee recommended that, in 1936, cinemas be permitted to show films on Sunday. There was one major stipulation—the picture *must* be "U" certificate. This was yet another nail in the horror movie's coffin.

The first of 1935's big horror movies to be trade shown in London was *Mark of the Vampire* (May 15), which was described as "Sensational! Soul-Stirring! and Spine Tingling!"

One of the many oddities in the career of Bela ("Dracula") Lugosi is that, although he was universally associated with the role, he only played the Count twice on screen. Despite *Dracula's* box office success and its role in creating the "horror movie," Universal did not produce a sequel for five years. When *Dracula's Daughter* was finally made, though, both Dracula and Lugosi were absent.

MGM, Hollywood's most prestigious studio, was no slouch at horror movies after *The Mask of Fu Manchu* and *Freaks*. The company decided to dust off the Lon Chaney silent *London After Midnight* (1927), giving the public a Dracular movie with—and without—Dracula.

In Visoka, a tiny Czechoslovakian village, Sir Karell Borotyn (Holmes Herbert) has been found dead, apparently the victim of a vampire, but Inspector Neumann (Lionel Atwill) is skeptical. A year later, the super-

Lionel Barrymore (as the crafty Professor Zelen) and friends in *Mark of the Vampire* **(1935).**

Luna (Carroll Borland) and Count Mora (Bela Lugosi)—a "vampire" (and supposedly inces-tuous) daughter and father in *Mark of the Vampire* (1935).

stitious villagers seem to be proven correct when two vampires, Count Mora (Bela Lugosi) and his daughter Luna (Carroll Borland), are seen stalking Borotyn Castle. Professor Zelen (Lionel Barrymore) is called in to investigate, and Sir Karell is soon discovered to be one of the undead, but all is not as it seems. Baron Otto (Jean Hersholt), who lusts after Irene Borotyn (Elizabeth Allan), killed her father and cleverly made it appear to be the work of a vampire. In order to frighten a confession out of Otto, Zelen hired two vaudeville performers—"The Count" and "Luna"—to play the vampires, convincing the easily spooked villain that his "victim" has returned.

Despite excellent atmosphere, outstanding production values, and a creepy performance by Lugosi, director Tod Browning's insistence on denying the supernatural by following the absurd premise of *London After Midnight* made *Mark of the Vampire* an interesting misfire. On the surface, there is nothing offensive about the picture other than its insulting climax. But, there is the matter of "Count Mora's" bullet wound. In the film's pre-cut version, the cause of the Count's "vampirism" is intoned by the village coroner (Egon Brecher): "He shot himself after he strangled his daughter." While this action was bad enough, its cause was originally far worse. Arthur Lenning (in *The Count*), related that scripter Guy Endore originally planned for the murder-suicide to be the result of an incestuous relationship.

Since Brecher's line was cut, and no hint of incest pervades the released version, viewers are on their own to figure things out. What is most disturbing about this "non-incestuous" event was that it was even considered in the first place.

However, both audiences and critics were unaware of the perversion that lurked beneath the surface of this slickly made picture. Following *Mark of the Vampire*'s London trade show, *The Kinematograph Weekly* (May 23, 1935) praised the film's "gripping story, grim, hair-raising thrills, good atmosphere, excellent teamwork by powerful cast, good title, and big exploitation angles." *Today's Cinema* (May 17) found the picture "ingenious" with "excellent technical qualities ... an excellent example of the 'horror' film." One can only imagine the reaction to Endore's *original* concept.

Trade shown one day after *Mark of the Vampire*, but with far less fanfare, was *WereWolf of London*, a seemingly tame horror entry, but with a few quirks of its own.

The picture begins with a presumption of "Darwinism" as fact ("Evolution was in a strange mood when this creation came along"). It should be remembered that the Scopes "monkey trial" had taken place a mere decade previously.

When testy Dr. Glendon—the WereWolf (Henry Hull)—fears that he might attack his wife Lisa (Valerie Hobson), he wants her to stay indoors during the full moon. But, she has other plans; reunited with her childhood sweetheart (Lester Matthews), she plans to go riding. "I shall ride tonight, tomorrow night, the next night."

732-P.8

Two Drs.—Glendon (Henry Hull) and Yogami (Warner Oland)—also two WereWolves in *WereWolf of London* (1935).

An odd triangle—husband and WereWolf (Henry Hull), wife (Valerie Hobson), and former boyfriend (Lester Matthews) in *WereWolf of London* (1935).

A secondary character took *his* vows even less seriously. A married zoo guard argues with his mistress. "I hadn't ought to do this—me with a wife and kids."

"But you don't love her," she says. "You love me. Oh, what a fool you are, a young fellow like you, tied to a white-faced scarecrow of a woman. You're going to leave her and come with me, ain't you?"

The fact that "the slut" is soon ravaged by the WereWolf does little to alleviate the scene's questionable morality—or the necessity of its inclusion in the movie.

Later that month, the long awaited sequel to *Frankenstein* was trade shown in London, awaited by both horror fans and local watch groups.

Bride of Frankenstein is among the most fondly remembered of all horror movies. Noted critic Leslie Halliwell (*Film Guide*) called it "the screen's most sophisticated masterwork of black comedy with all the talents working deftly to one end. Every scene has its own delights and they

British censors were outraged by *Bride of Frankenstein* (1935) despite touching moments like this one between the Monster (Boris Karloff) and the Blind Hermit (O.P. Heggie).

are woven together into a superb, if willful, cinematic narrative which, of its gentle mocking kind, has never been surpassed."

This is the popular view, echoed in countless reviews and commentaries. Everything about *Bride of Frankenstein* screams quality, and the modern viewer is just as easily drawn into the fairy-tale plot as his predecessors.

After Mary Shelley (Elsa Lanchester) explains that she wrote *Frankenstein* as a morality play, she reveals to her husband Percy (Douglas Walton) that the monster (Boris Karloff) survived the burning windmill. His creator, Henry Frankenstein (Colin Clive), while being nursed by Elizabeth (Valerie Hobson), is confronted by the mad Dr. Pretorius (Ernest Thesiger). He attempts to seduce the weak-willed Henry into helping him create a race of artificial beings by making a mate for the

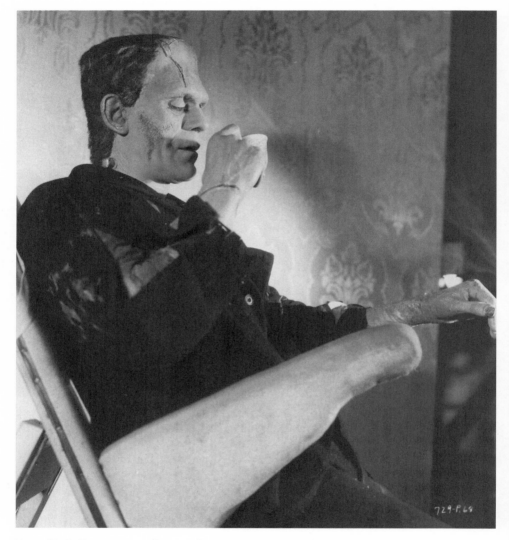

Boris Karloff, at peace on the set of *Bride of Frankenstein* **(1935), blissfully unaware of bans to come.**

monster. After wreaking havoc among the villagers, the monster is humanized by a blind hermit (O.P. Heggie) but his brief idyll is destroyed by a group of hunters. On the run, the monster encounters Pretorius body-snatching in a crypt, and the two join forces to convince the reluctant Henry to continue. After Elizabeth's abduction, Henry agrees and creates a female (Elsa Lanchester) who rejects her suitor. Anguished, the monster frees Henry and Elizabeth, then destroys Pretorius, his intended, and (presumably) himself.

But, for all of its "gentle mocking" and cinematic fireworks, *Bride of Frankenstein* has a seldom mentioned dark side that did not go unnoticed by contemporary critics. While these "objectional" scenes may be viewed as harmless today, they crossed several lines of thirties taste and had censors—especially in the United Kingdom—reaching for their scissors. Driven by director James Whale's odd sense of humor, the movie was intended to be an "in-joke," but Hollywood Production Code head Joseph Breen was not laughing.

Chief among Breen's objections were Whale's inclusion of religion as part of the joke. Despite the disclaimer in the campy prologue that puts the story's "morality" on parade, Breen felt that just the opposite was taking place. His office insisted that Universal delete any comparisons between Frankenstein and God before the script could be passed. How Breen missed the infamous crucifixion parody, with the monster standing in as Christ, is not certain.

Homosexuality was a strict taboo in the post–Code films of the thirties, yet Whale managed to sneak in an apparently gay character. Ernest Thesiger's Dr. Pretorius, described in *Time* as a "scruffy fag," lures the confused Henry Frankenstein—literally—from his marriage bed after ordering Elizabeth from her own bedroom. Pretorius then introduces Henry to an "alternative form" of procreation—minus women—and Elizabeth is quickly forgotten. Even more incredible is the inclusion of necrophilia, when the monster, entering a crypt, caresses the face of a female corpse while muttering "Friend?" Pretorius' lackey (Dwight Frye) later refers to a corpse as a "pretty little thing in her way." The monster soon intones, "I love dead ... hate living" for those who missed the point. The movie's subversive view might best be summarized when Pretorius, while playing with a miniature Satan he created, muses, "Sometimes I have wondered if life wouldn't be much more amusing if we were all devils and no nonsense about angels or being good." These scenes might well be considered "good clean fun" by today's standards, but many in the mid-thirties were not amused despite the film's success with the public.

Bride of Frankenstein (budgeted at almost $300,000), began production on January 2, 1935, and was completed on March 7. It opened at New York's Roxy on May 9 to wildly enthusiastic business and reviews. The Pantages Theater in Los Angeles played the film 11 times daily to accommodate the crowds.

Bride of Frankenstein's huge American success did not escape notice in the UK. *The Kinematograph Weekly* (May 23) enthused over "waiting lines a block long at the Orpheum in San Francisco." Reviews from the United States had also been encouraging, and cinema owners, no doubt, were licking their chops.

The first sign that something was going wrong may have been *Today's Cinema's* (May 30) review following an early trade show. "Direction, production, staging, and general treatment effects decided improvement on original film but carries bloodchilling, horrific incident trifle too far ... prologue in execrable taste ... sensation is carried a little beyond reasonable limits. *Bride of Frankenstein is* not a pleasant type of entertainment one would recommend." This was an exceedingly harsh judgment from a usually easily pleased source.

Meanwhile, *WereWolf of London* was winning rave reviews in prerelease; general release was set for November 11. "This is the goods!" (*Bristol Evening Post*); "A triumph!" (*The Star*); "Grisly and gruesome, gorgeous, and enjoyable!" (*Sunday Referee*); "Just the kind of thing to see" (*Birmingham Post*); and "Don't fail to see it!" (*Jewish Daily Post*). *Bride of Frankenstein* would soon get its share of rave reviews, and would also soon be banned.

Its premiere was set for June 27 at the Strand Tivoli, and was attended by royalty—the Duke and Duchess of Kent (who reportedly enjoyed the film). Elsa Lanchester was there, too, as was the press, which enthused: "Brilliantly set—it is wonderful!" (*Daily Herald*); "Fantasy run riot. Interesting entertainment" (*Daily Sketch*); "One of the finest episodes of macabre miming" (*Daily Express*); "Highly diverting" (*Daily Mirror*); "A wonderful job" (*Evening Telegraph*); "Eerie, grim, and staggering!" (*Sunday Times*); "Impressive and powerful" (*Sunday Referee*); "Highbrows will be amused, lowbrows will be entertained." General release was set for September 30, and exhibitors held their breath.

The new Hollywood Production Code, headed by Will Hays and Joseph Breen, was beginning to make its presence felt in the UK. In June 1935, Hays wrote to the Federation of British Industries, offering to test the status of British films under the Code. "In accordance with the action," wrote Hays, "arrangements will be made to provide such amplifications of personnel and facilities of the Production Code Administration as may be needed in order that the services shall be provided for the examination of submitted scripts and pictures similar to those which have been established in Hollywood" (*Today's Cinema*, June 24, 1935).

As if on cue, *Bride of Frankenstein* premiered at the London Tivoli

Boris Karloff (as Bateman), clearly outclassed by Bela Lugosi's Dr. Vollin in *The Raven* **(1935).**

on July 1, with September 30 set as its general release. British critics went mad with praise: "It is wonderful—brilliantly set" (*Daily Herald*); "Karloff is colossally fine—eerie, grim, and staggering" (*Sunday Times*); "Played, produced, and directed in exactly the right spirit demanded by a thriller" (*News of the World*); "General appeal very good" (*Lancashire Daily Post*); "This picture is ENTERTAINMENT" (*Morning Advertiser*); "A brilliant picture" (*The Star*); and "An amazing spectacle. A wonderful example of cinema technique" (*Reynolds News*).

Today's Cinema (July 2) called *Bride of Frankenstein*, "The best sequel ever screened," which may be even more true today than in 1935. "Public reaction to the picture has been excellent," the paper reported. "The crowds have been lavish with their applause and enthusiasm." Even the Duke and Duchess of Kent were impressed. While London cinemagoers were courting the *Bride*, an ominous black bird swooped into the picture—*The Raven* was to be trade shown on July 16. It was described, generously, as "differing entirely from *Bride of Frankenstein*." Few would argue that point.

The Raven is among the most notorious of the thirties shockers and is often given "credit" for single-handedly creating the British horror ban. While there may be some small truth to this, it is more likely that *The Raven* just happened to be the proverbial last straw. After the British censors' outrage at *Bride of Frankenstein*'s "necrophilia and blasphemy," *The Raven*, with its own form of blasphemy mixed with sadism and torture, was just too much for the market to bear.

Jean Thatcher (Irene Ware), a young dancer, is seriously injured in a car wreck. Frantic, her father, Judge Thatcher (Samuel S. Hinds), and her fiancé, Dr. Halden (Lester Matthews), seek the help of reclusive surgeon Dr. Vollin (Bela Lugosi). Vollin has retired from practice and spends his days gratifying his obsession with Edgar Allan Poe. After being told that he is the only one who can save Jean, he grudgingly consents to do the surgery and soon becomes obsessed with her. After her recovery, Jean performs an interpretive dance of Poe's "The Raven"—a tribute which Vollin mistakes for love. When the judge senses Vollin's interest, he forbids him to see her. Maddened, Vollin plans revenge.

His plan takes form when Bateman (Boris Karloff), an escaped criminal, begs Vollin to surgically alter his face so he can avoid capture. He does, turning Bateman into a monster. Bateman reluctantly agrees to help Vollin in exchange for being made "normal" again. During a party at Vollin's estate (foolishly attended by the Thatchers and Halden), Bateman abducts the judge and fastens him to a torture device copied from Poe's "The Pit and the Pendulum." Vollin places Jean and Halden in a room with compressing walls, but the now soft-hearted Bateman balks. While freeing the couple, Bateman is mortally wounded but manages to force Vollin into the death room. The couple frees the judge as Vollin is crushed by his own device.

"Dear Sir (or Madam)," smirked the Universal pressbook. "We feel that your students will be interested in seeing on the screen a remarkable entertainment inspired by Edgar Allan Poe's literary classic, "The Raven." The great writer's lines are frequently quoted throughout the picture, and you and your students will feel a new interest and appreciate more keenly the dramatic power of this famous verse."

Yes… the film was being sold as an aid to education! It is fortunate for Universal after *(Murders in the Rue Morgue, The Black Cat,* and *The Raven)* that poor Poe left no heirs. If he had, they certainly would have owned Universal after the lawsuits. It is sad to think of the multitudes who, after seeing these pictures without having read anything by Poe, must have felt the great writer to be on the level of a comic book scribbler.

For those horror fans of the *"Famous Monsters* generation," *The Raven*

Judge Thatcher (Samuel S. Hinds) menaced by Bateman (Boris Karloff) in *The Raven* (1935).

was first introduced to us on its pages as a "classic." It had to be, with Karloff, Bela ("Dracula") Lugosi, released by Universal in the thirties. Actually, the film is a mess. Boris Karloff gives what is one of his worst performances for Universal, hampered by the usually brilliant Jack Pierce's sloppy makeup; poor Bateman's disfigured eye looks like a hardened fried egg laid on his cheek. Lugosi is way over the top, but easily steals, for once, a film from his "rival." The picture, compared to *The Black Cat* and *Bride of Frankenstein*, looks cheap and hurried, but the real problem here is that *The Raven*, despite its "classic" status, has very little to offer. One of the few interesting things about the picture is, despite its theme and reputation, only the two villains die—no other characters are killed.

The Raven premiered on July 4, 1935, at New York's Roxy to decent crowds and indignant reviewers. The film contained a number of upsetting lines. "You're not only a great surgeon, but a great musician too," fawns Miss Thatcher to Vollin. "Extraordinary man—you're almost not a man ... almost ... a God?" Vollin modestly suggests. Or, how about Bateman's excuse for an inexcusable act of violence? "I told him to keep his mouth shut," Bateman whines, "but he gets the gag out and starts yelling for the police. I had the acetylene torch in my hand." "So," asks Vollin, interested, "you put the burning torch into his face... into his eyes?" Bateman, head hanging, mumbles, "Well, sometimes you can't help things like that." Adding to the unhealthy mix are torture and Dr. Vollin's sexual interest in a woman young enough to be his own daughter.

The Raven is far less objectionable than *Island of Lost Souls, Murders in the Rue Morgue,* or *The Black Cat*; it merely *seems* worse because it is so ineptly done. As Karloff resorts to falling back on *Frankenstein*-like growls and hand gestures, it becomes painfully obvious that this picture is no more than an exercise in sadism minus imagination.

Universal *may* have been aware of what it had wrought; the pressbook suggested that the following disclaimer was to be placed in theatre lobbies. "WARNING! In keeping with this theatre's policy of frankness, WE WARN YOU that this is a picture of the wild shocker type. Highly nervous, timid people should stay away." Typical pressbook hype? Of course, but with more truth than Universal may have realized.

Bela Lugosi appeared at the Prince Edward trade show; he would soon return to the United States after appearing in Hammer's *Mystery of the Mary Celeste*. Even this courtesy did not spare *The Raven*. *Today's Cinema* (July 18) was unimpressed. "Here is a film which definitely sets out to chill the blood and scarify the nerves. Whether it can be considered to succeed depends rather upon the type of patron that views it as for some, subtle suggestion is better than lurid overstatement. A grim idea that is not without interest, it is here a trifle too melodramatic. Lurid entertainment for non-squeamish patrons."

Sight and Sound (August) agreed: "This deliberately horrific film takes its inspiration and a good deal of its material, not so much, as stated, from *The Raven*, with its sense of somber mystery, but rather from the torture aspects of the *Tales of Mystery, Imagination, and Horror*, two of which are woven into the story. ...For those who thrill to horror there are thrills enough; but one audience reacted, at times, as horror was piled upon horror, with the laughter of emotional self-defense. There is too much of Poe's horror and not enough of his imagination for the film to be considered as more than moderate, either from the box office or the artistic point of view." *The Kinematograph Weekly* (July 25) described *The Raven* as a "Macabre melodrama; an attempt to incorporate many of the eerie thrills to be found in Edgar Allan Poe's stories into one big thriller. But without the author's narrative skill to hold the plot together, the film becomes just another manufactured hair raiser with the established stooges of crime entertainment, Lugosi and Karloff, putting over the same old act. But, as good as these experienced players are, they find it difficult to prevent the extravagant situations from being greeted with laughter."

Non-film related journals, however, were not laughing. *The London Times* (August 4) offered:

> Last week, so the publicity men told us, was an All-Murder Week. Every picture should have a purpose, preferably a high one. Any concentration upon Murder as Murder can only kill the films themselves. But it is difficult to speculate as to what intention, other than the stimulation of a low morbid interest, can be behind such a production as *The Raven*, at the Capitol. Here is a film of "horror" for "horror's" sake. It exploits degrading abnormalities of human nature. It devises shelter under the statement that it has been inspired by the genius of Edgar Allan Poe. Nonsense. Neither story nor treatment give indication of any imaginative control. To suggest that there is the slightest affinity between the creation of his powerful and extraordinary mind and this sordid and bungling work is sheer charlatism. Shock follows shock but the effect is only to nauseate those with weak stomachs and provoke laughter in those with strong ones. Louis Friedlander's direction concentrates on visual and tangible frightfulness to the entire exclusion of subtlety. What artistic merit or legitimate entertainment value there may be in films of this kind I leave others to discover. Their capacity for harm would seem apparent to anyone. Certain mentalities are susceptible to morbid appeal. They will not resist these examples.

The Daily Express (August 4) concurred. "Author Edgar Allan Poe, on whose work this film is based, was fond of graves but he would turn in his own if he could see this Universal 'masterpiece.' It is a shocker staged in an all-electric torture chamber... its horror is revolting. I thought the censor had put his foot down on horror films of this kind? Apparently not."

The Express (August 4) joined in the fray. "It is true that there is a reading of Poe's poem, but that is all there is to remind us of him. Like any chamber of horrors, there is neither life nor horror in this film. There is an occasional touch of the grotesque and one of the physically repulsive."

The situation was not much better on the "other side," either. Greg Mank reported (in *Karloff and Lugosi*) that, as in the UK, individual local communities in the United States rose up in protest: New York and Ohio ordered cuts of Samuel S. Hinds under the pendulum and Lugosi's line, "Torture waiting, waiting. It will be sweet, Judge Thatcher." Karloff's line about burning the man's eyes with a blowtorch was cut in Pennsylvania. Canada was not amused, either. British Columbia banned *The Raven* outright until it was re-edited, Quebec cut the blowtorch lines, and Alberta removed several shots of Karloff's face. *The Raven* was completely banned in Ontario, and, back across the pond, the Netherlands did likewise.

The New York Times (July 5, 1935) laid it on the line, headlining its reviews, "A Horror Film in More Ways Than One," and proceeded to take to task not only the movie but Universal. "Suddenly there comes a tapping, as of someone gently rapping. ...But there will be no gentle rapping from the corner of the curious photoplay which Universal, with amazing effrontery, describes as having been inspired by two Edgar Allan Poe classics. [It is] the season's worst horror film—a fatal mistake from beginning to end. Lugosi and Karloff try hard, even though, both being cultured men, they must have suffered at the indignity being visited upon the helpless Edgar Allan Poe. If *The Raven* is the best Universal can do with one of the greatest horror story writers of all time, then it better stick with the pulpies for plot material!"

This last point was well made. Then (as now) there were only so many worthwhile horror stories to be adapted as movies and, by 1935, most of them had been used. What remained were sequels and unsatisfactory adaptations of properties, like *The Raven*, that were unsuitable in the first place. The horror genre was quickly running out of gas and might have sputtered to a halt even if the UK had not become militant.

Horror fans, from 1931 to 1935, had seen film adaptations of novels (*Dracula*), plays (*Dr. X*), sequels (*Bride of Frankenstein*), remakes (*Mark of the Vampire*), and originals (*WereWolf of London*). By 1935, there was really nowhere to go.

While *Bride of Frankenstein* and *The Raven* were awaiting their general release, one of the most extraordinary horror pictures of all was trade shown at the Prince Edward. Peter Lorre, in his U.S. film debut, arrived

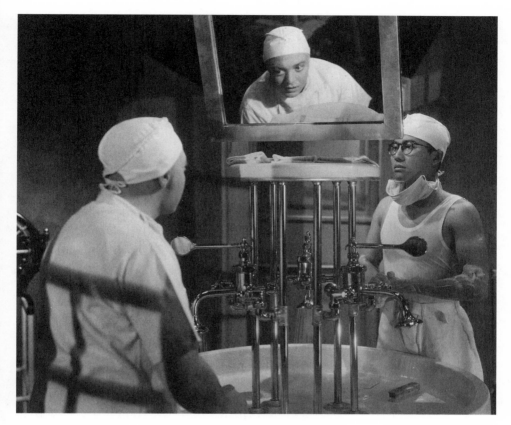

Dr. Gogol (Peter Lorre) scrubs up while Dr. Wong (Keye Luke) looks on in *Mad Love* (1935).

on the London screen on April 7 in *Hands of Orlac* (U.S. title—*Mad Love*). Lorre had earlier created a sensation in both the United States and Britain in the German *M* (1931), a horrifying study of child molestation and murder. Although not-by-definition a "horror movie," it could have received an horrific advisory. Instead, the BBFC passed it, greatly cut, with an "A." In *Hands of Orlac*, Lorre was even more sensational.

Dr. Gogol (Lorre), a respected surgeon, frequents Paris' Théâtre des Horreurs due to his perverted fascination for its star Yvonne Orlac (Frances Drake). Faithfully married to Stephen (Colin Clive), a famous pianist, she is repulsed when Gogol confronts her with his passion. Spurned, he buys a wax figure of Yvonne as a "replacement." When Stephen's hands are crushed in a train accident, Yvonne influences Gogol to intervene. He replaces Orlac's useless hands with those of Rollo

(Edward Brophy)—an executed knife murderer. When Stephen remains unable to resume his career, he disintegrates mentally, and Gogol sees his opportunity. After knifing Orlac's estranged stepfather, Gogol masquerades as Rollo, who claims that Gogol sewed his head back on. Orlac is convinced that he murdered his stepfather while under the influence of Rollo's hands. Stephen is arrested, but Yvonne suspects Gogol and breaks into his apartment. "Disguised" as the wax effigy, she confounds Gogol who thinks his desire has brought it to life. Realizing her deception, Gogol tries to kill her, but Stephen, who has arrived with the police, dispatches him with a knife.

Despite (or because of) Peter Lorre's perverse portrayal, the picture was not embraced by audiences. The American *Motion Picture Herald* called *Mad Love* after its August 2 release, "the picture that makes a manager want to hide from view—the type of picture that brought about censorship." *Today's Cinema* (August 9) was provisional in its praise. "First class entertainment of its type. *Hands of Orlac* may not prove to the taste of patrons. Not a film for the squeamish." *Sight and Sound* (August) found *Hands of Orlac* to be "quite unsuitable for children and nervous people." Few would disagree.

By the summer of 1935, the horror movie in the UK was in serious trouble, under attack from all sides. The July 4 *Kinematograph Weekly* provided no independence for horror films as a headline screamed "Censor Attacks Horror and Gangster Pictures." Edward Shortt, president of the British Board of Film Censors, questioned the desirability of importing horror and gangster movies into Britain. Shortt was committed to keeping the cinema a place of family entertainment. "The standard of film censorship," he said, "must be somewhat different from those required in other forms of public entertainment which cater, at the most, to thousands, whereas films are catering to millions. Taking these factors into consideration, I came to the conclusion that it would be wrong for the Board to certify any film which offends a reasonable number of reasonably minded people. Some films, particularly some emanating from America, have been too far in advance of public opinion in the outlook and daringness."

During 1934, 1,862 films were shown in the UK. Of these, 466 received an "A" certificate, and 1,396 a "U." However, the trend toward graphic violence and sex in Hollywood was making the "U-A" method unworkable. "First and foremost," Shortt said, "there appears to be a tendency towards an increase in the number of films which come within the horror classification which I think is unfortunate and undesirable."

In 1934, four movies were classified as "horror," but, by mid–1935, five had already been so labeled. Shortt considered these films to be unsuitable for children no matter if they were accompanied by an adult. "Although a separate category has been established for these films," he said, "I am sorry to learn they are on the increase, as I cannot believe such films are wholesome, pandering as they do to the love of the morbid and horrible. Although there is little chance of children seeing these films, I believe they will have a deleterious effect on the adolescent. I hope that producers and renters will accept this word of warning and discourage this type of subject as far as possible."

For those wise enough to hear it, this point marked the end of the horror movie in Britain. A week later, the clerk to the Birmingham Justices announced that *The Raven*, recently trade shown in London, would have to pass a local screening board before it could be publicly shown.

Boris Karloff was again on the British screen in one of his greatest performances, playing both Anton and Gregor deBerghman in *The Black Room*. Although not strictly a "horror movie," the Karloff name made it one. Columbia, sensing the volatile situation, carefully advertised the picture as "Not a Horrific." Premiering at the Pavilion on August 26, *The Black Room* was described in *Today's Cinema* (September 4) as a "period melodrama [with] ... sinister evil ... sudden death ... [and] fraternal hatred." The clever tale of twins, one good (Anton), one evil (Gregor), gave Karloff one of his best acting opportunities. Graham Greene (*The Spectator*, September 20) enthused, "Mr. Boris Karloff has been allowed to act at last. The direction is good; it has caught, as Mr. James Whale never did with *Frankenstein*, the genuine Gothic note." The film also had an odd sexual undertone. Gregor eyes a young beauty (Katherine DeMille) as he eats a pear. "A pear's the best fruit," he intones. "There's lots of juice in a pear. I like the feel of a pear, and when you're through with it"—he takes a huge bite and tosses it away, his message clear. Unfortunately, the dissipated nobleman does more than toss away unwanted young girls—he kills them. Gregor momentarily escapes his well-deserved fate by murdering his kindly twin and impersonating him. The picture lacked any supernatural content or graphic violence, but its grim premise of twin vs. twin, and Karloff's brilliantly unsettling performance, nudged it closer to the horror genre than, perhaps, Columbia wished it to go.

The Home Office released this statement on September 12, 1935: "In other parts of the country—in the smaller areas—there is a feeling that the censor has been too lax. London may sometimes think the censor too

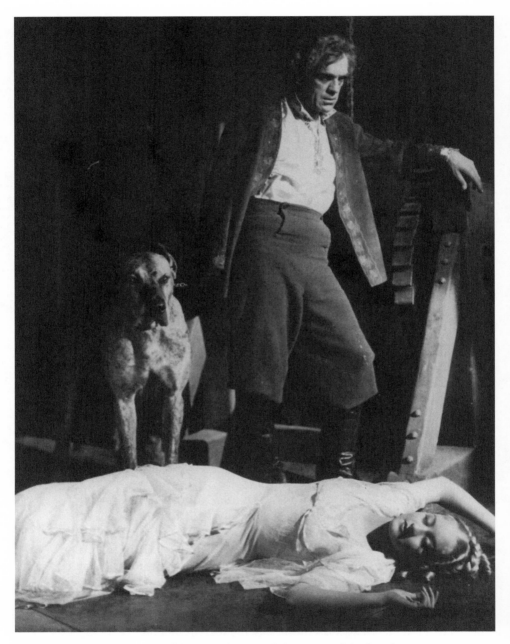

Boris Karloff as Gregor, one of the most dissipated characters of the decade in *The Black Room* (1935).

strict. Generally speaking, the nation as a whole approves of the censorship and the way it is carrying out its duties. If any change is called for, it lies not so much in any alteration or addition to film censorship as in some method of dealing with the exploitation of certain films. If that happens, it will be the fault of the trade for not restraining (itself) within decent limits." One need not think too hard to imagine to which "certain films" the Home Office was referring.

Then, a bombshell was dropped. Less than two weeks before its scheduled release, the most "beloved" of all horror movies was banned. "It was officially announced that *Bride of Frankenstein* will not be publicly screened in Birmingham," reported the *Kinematograph Weekly* (September 19). "This is the outcome of a private viewing of the film at the Gaumont Palace attended by members of the Public Entertainment Committee." The public was not amused, as illustrated by an irate writer to the *Birmingham Daily Mail*. "With all due respect to the Committee and its ban on *Bride of Frankenstein*, one wonders how much longer the Birmingham citizen will put up with being smacked and put to bed. Why should I have to go outside the city to see *Bride of Frankenstein*, a picture passed by the British Board of Film Censors and has been shown with great success in London?" In order to *be* passed, *Bride of Frankenstein* suffered several cuts, including Karloff's corpse-caressing.

A common cry heard throughout Britain in 1935 came from cinema managers: "We want better quality films to show and will show them whenever they are available." This "quality," however, had little to do with acting, writing, or photographic skill; in this context, *Bride of Frankenstein*, for example, was clearly a desirable picture. The fact that film craftsmanship was being so easily dismissed by those concerned only with content was a matter of great concern to those inside the British film industry.

The greatest fear continued to be government intervention, as addressed in a pointed editorial (*The Kinematograph Weekly*, October 14): "A very influential body, much of whose work is done behind closed doors, has decided to take a hand in the matter of film censorship. The County Councils Association is to be approached by the Surrey C.C. Licensing Committee and asked to take steps to secure that the Consultative Committee should 'examine films on behalf of all licensing authorities and advise.' This, if successful, will mean no less than the supercession of the British Board of Film Censors and the final result of that action can hardly be foreseen, except that it must almost certainly be disastrous. Its members, however well meaning and unbiased, are distinctly out of touch with the masses, and it is the masses to whom the cinema screen administers its weekly or bi-weekly entertainment."

Why *Bride of Frankenstein* was subjected to extensive local banning while pictures of lesser quality but more blatancy (*Murders in the Zoo*) went relatively unnoticed is not certain. One possibility is that the general theme of Frankenstein-as-God was found to be more offensive than more down to earth horrors. It is worth noting that *Bride of Frankenstein* experienced little opposition in London. In early October, the London County Council addressed the censorship issue, stating that "No film shall be exhibited which has not been passed by the Board"; yet, significantly, the provinces were banning those the Board had certified.

"HORROR FILMS AGAIN" was a sarcastic headline in *Today's Cinema* (November 2), and *Bride of Frankenstein* was its subject. The Cornwall-Devon branch of the CEA was taken to task for banning the *Bride* too close to its presentation. James Saunders, circuit supervisor for Gaumont Cinemas, wrote to the committee: "We had this film booked for the week commencing Monday, October 14, and, as you are probably aware, the authorities at the last moment banned its exhibition. We cannot complain in regard to the right of the Watch Committee in connection with the banning, but what we do feel is that we are entitled to a longer notice than that given to us."

Mr. Saunders received little sympathy. He was told that since two (unnamed) "horrifics" had previously been locally banned, he should have expected the same treatment for *Bride of Frankenstein*. H.J. Watkins, of the St. Austell Cinema, questioned why the picture was exhibited without comment in nearby Plymouth. He was told that "feeling in regard to certain films varies in various areas." I.W. Crewes of Exeter volunteered that, since *Frankenstein* had been locally banned, one should have expected the same for its sequel. Mr. Watkins felt that, to protect cinema owners, a "universal decision" on horror movies was needed as opposed to "the decisions of individuals in different parts of the country."

The result of this haphazard banning was that cinema owners had a good reason not to book horror pictures.

Four days later, Ralph Bromhead chaired a meeting of the London County Council to discuss "horrifics." Two major points were made. Children should not, under any circumstances, be in attendance, and that the committee was adamantly opposed to the future production of horror movies.

Bride of Frankenstein ran into more problems on November 13 when the Caernarvonshire Stage Plays Committee addressed whether the picture should be shown. Local cinema owners complained about the wasted expense of advertising a film that was later banned, and the chairman agreed that this was a poor business practice. However, when Universal offered a print of the *Bride* for the committee to view before passing judgment, the offer was declined.

The CEA meeting on November 21, once again dealt with horror movies and their attendance by children. The London Branch again felt that children should not attend "horrifics" even with a parent, and, in another death blow to the genre, suggested that members "should try to keep their programmes free from horror films" (*Today's Cinema*, November 22). One week later, the Surrey County Council made the same recommendations.

The CEA again leapt into action on December 13, when a letter was drafted stating its opposition to horror film production. Copies of the letter were to be sent to the appropriate American producers and to major cinema owners in the UK as the gloves continued to be taken off.

The Middlesex County Council was next, announcing on December 19, that children would be unilaterally banned from all pictures deemed "horrific" by the council regardless of the BBFC certification. "A small number of pictures," the report read (*Today's Cinema*, December 20), "have been produced which are generally accepted as unsuitable for exhibition to children on account of their terrifying nature. Your committee first considered the question of the exhibition of these films in 1932 in connection with the film *Frankenstein*. Your committee's attention has now been called to the increasing number of these films which have recently been issued. Your committee has formed the opinion that films of this nature should not be seen at all by children."

With children virtually barred from horror movies, cinema owners were asking themselves why they should even book them.

1936 — Steps
Have Been Taken

As 1936 dawned, Universal was still going through the motions of continuing its horror series, apparently the last to know that the genre was dead. On January 2, *Today's Cinema* announced the impending arrival of *The Invisible Ray* ("secrecy surrounded all studio activities"), *Dracula's Daughter* ("the most brilliant of its type, the limit in breathtaking thrills"), *Bluebeard*, to star Boris Karloff, and remakes of *The Hunchback of Notre Dame* and *The Phantom of the Opera*, both with "all star casts." In addition, Concordia Films, a British company, announced that director Robert Wiene was to remake his 1919 classic *Cabinet of Dr. Caligari*— another failed project which joined the three above.

The sticky issue of children and "A" films continued to be a problem, as the Hendon Education Committee planned a joint conference on the subject involving the Middlesex, London, and Surrey County Councils. The HEC was concerned about a rise in juvenile delinquency and, naturally, blamed the movies the miscreants may or may not have seen. "Some people think there should be no censorship," said Sir Cecil Levita, chairman of the Film Censorship Committee (*Today's Cinema*, January 6), "others, that it should be stricter. Censorship is essentially a matter of opinion and all one can do is to take a mean course."

Michael Balcon, who founded Gainsborough Pictures and produced many of Alfred Hitchcock's early pictures (including *The Lodger*, 1926, and *The Man Who Knew Too Much*, 1934) was becoming concerned that the attacks on horror movies could spread to "thrillers," and felt that "it might be advisable to arrive at some definition of the meaning of 'horrific'

126

Dr. Rukh (Boris Karloff) inspects his Radium X-poisoned hands in *The Invisible Ray* (1936).

as opposed to those of the 'thriller' description," he said (*Today's Cinema*, January 10), obviously concerned about his ace director's status.

Universal unleashed *The Invisible Ray* in London at a February 10 trade show at the Palace. "Among the most novel of the year—nerve tingling thrills, unique, powerful, weird!" claimed the press release. Boris Karloff and Bela Lugosi were teamed for the third time, with Karloff in his "first straight role" (*Today's Cinema*, February 5). This comment was obviously made by someone who missed, among others, *Scarface* (1932), *The Lost Patrol*, and *The House of Rothschild* (both 1934). Universal was quick to point out in its advertising that *The Invisible Ray* was not a horror picture; actually, it was a charming example of early science fiction.

Dr. Janos Rukh (Karloff), a reclusive scientist living in the Carpathians with his wife Diana (Frances Drake) and blind mother (Violet Kemble Cooper), is visited by a team of his more orthodox colleagues who have come to witness Rukh's new discovery. He has determined that a new element, Radium X, was part of a meteor that landed in Africa centuries before. The A team is assembled—Dr. Benet (Lugosi), Sir Francis Stevens (Walter Kingsford), Lady Arabella Stevens (Beulah Bondi), her nephew Ronald (Frank Lawton), and Diana—and off they go. Rukh becomes poisoned, in both mind and body, by the powerful material and his very touch becomes deadly. Convinced that everyone is against him (and, since Lady Arabella tries to get Ronald and Diana together, he may have been right), he goes on a murderous rampage. After restoring his mother's sight with the Radium X, she destroys the counteractive designed by Benet to keep Janos alive. Rukh bursts into flames as he jumps from a window.

Today's Cinema (February 12) described *The Invisible Ray* as a "scientific melodrama, off-beaten-track entertainment of popular pattern. Boris Karloff makes a curiously sympathetic figure of the stricken Rukh, again ably supported by Lugosi." While Karloff and Universal were basking in this faint praise, a ghost from the recent past returned to haunt them: *Bride of Frankenstein* was again under attack.

Sir Archibald Bodkin, head of Licensing Sessions, was concerned about the type of movies playing at two cinemas under his jurisdiction—the Radway and Grand in Sidmouth. "Perhaps I ought not to put my private views before you," he said modestly (*Today's Cinema*, February 19), "but will you remember the justices will be very careful as to the type of films that will be shown." Mr. A.W. Ellis, manager of the cinemas, was planning to show *Bride of Frankenstein* which had recently been banned in Exeter. Ellis was uncertain on what grounds it had been banned, but said in his defense it had been "passed for adults and no children were allowed to see it. It had not been banned everywhere."

When asked by Sir Archibald if he felt the picture was fit to be seen in Sidmouth, Ellis replied, "I think it is desirable for people who like that kind of entertainment, and people who do not like it need not go."

Ellis' intelligent remark had little effect on Sir Archibald, who countered with, "It will be interesting to see who does go. Only really good films should be exhibited, and not those horrific films. Is there not something a little more sensible, educational, and refined than some of those American things that are shown?"

Sir Archibald granted Ellis his license, but felt *Bride of Frankenstein* should be shown to local justices so they could decide if the picture was worthy of exhibition. An underlying problem also surfaced—Ellis was under fire for showing too many *American* made movies!

While this fiasco unfolded, Boris Karloff was signed for three Universal pictures for 1936-37, and arrived in the UK aboard the *Washington* to begin two British films.

On February 19, the Home Office sat down to discuss the Hendon Education Committee's proposal and film censorship in general. This meeting was closely watched by all concerned; nine days earlier, the House of Commons had been treated to a similar meeting. Just when it seemed that nothing more could go wrong for the horror movie, the bottom fell out—the genre's creator was destroyed.

Universal Pictures, Hollywood's most famous producer of horror movies, was founded by Carl Laemmle, a German immigrant, in 1912. His sprawling Universal City, 230 acres in the San Fernando Valley, was built in 1915 and, by the thirties, the studio fell somewhere between the "majors" (MGM) and the "minors" (RKO). Although its pictures lacked the gloss and stars of the majors, Universal had more than its share of success—especially with the horror classics.

Unfortunately, the generally negative effects of the Depression, plus Laemmle's penchant for hiring *lots* of family members to do nothing, added to a devastating strike that left the company reeling by 1933. Laemmle began fielding—and rejecting—bailout offers and finally, on November 1, 1935, he borrowed a million dollars to keep Universal afloat. The money came from the Standard Capital Corporation, headed by J. Cheever Cowdin, and from Charles R. Rogers. Both had an option to buy Universal for $5.5 million within a three-month period. Laemmle lost the gamble that the receipts of his pictures currently in release would cover the loan and, on March 4, 1936, Standard Capital took over. "Uncle Carl" resigned and died three years later.

Universal's British holdings were taken over by General Film Distributors for £1,225,000—the biggest deal in British film history to that date. A syndicate headed by C.M. Woolf, Lord Portal, J. Arthur Rank, Paul Lindenberg, and L.W. Farrow negotiated with Standard Capital. The deal was viewed as a boon to both the British film industry and to the Anglo-American trade balance. It was also another nail in the horror movies' coffin.

"The New Universal" was now headed by Cowdin, Rogers, and Robert H. Cochrane, an original founder. One of their first actions was to move out over 70 Laemmles, including Carl Jr. The next step was to concentrate on "family entertainment" like Deanna Durbin musicals. Rogers, *not* a horror fan, closed the lid on their production after the release of the already completed *Dracula's Daughter*. A Karloff-Lugosi property, *The Electric Man*, was the first casualty; it resurfaced in 1941 as *Man Made Monster* with Lon Chaney, Jr., and Lionel Atwill.

Charles Rogers soon discovered that "family entertainment" was not for all families and, after a desultory two years, resigned on May 19, 1938. Pictures like *As Good as Married* and *Breezing Home* made no one forget *Dracula* and *Frankenstein*. He was replaced by RKO's Cliff Work. By the time the British horror ban was instituted on January 1, 1937, it no longer mattered; Hollywood was no longer interested in making horrors.

Lost in the shuffle of the Universal sale was the banning of *Hands of Orlac* by the Northampton Watch Committee on March 2. Individual horror movies would be banned by individual authorities with regularity throughout the year. *The Raven* was the next to go when a local censor in Rotherham, South Yorkshire, refused to allow its exhibition. *The WereWolf of London* had been banned there in February to little avail; typically, the picture played just down the road in Sheffield.

On April 16, Carl Laemmle issued a farewell to the British moviegoing public. "Moving pictures have been my life work for thirty years," he said (*Today's Cinema*, April 17). "I have tried so to conduct Universal that, when I left it, the industry would feel that I had done more for the business than it has done for me."

Warner Bros.' *The Walking Dead*, which gave Boris Karloff one of his most sympathetic horror roles, was trade shown on April 22. *Today's Cinema* (April 24) called the picture a "resuscitation melodrama," not a "horror movie."

John Ellman (Karloff), an ex-con, is framed for the murder of Judge Shaw (Joseph King) by the real culprits—a group of racketeers headed by Nolan (Ricardo Cortez), a shady lawyer. Due to Nolan's non-existent defense strategy, Ellman is electrocuted. He is restored to life by Dr. Beaumont (Edmund Gwenn) after Nancy (Marguerite Churchill) and Jimmy (Warren Hull), who witnessed the murder, reveal the truth. Ellman becomes an avenging angel and, one by one, uses the gang's fears to decimate them. After meting out justice, Ellman dies, bathed in a heavenly glow, in a cemetery.

This Warner Bros. production could just as easily have been a gangster story and was presented in a *film noir* style by Michael Curtiz, the studio's master of all genres. The picture was released in the UK minus Karloff's death cell scenes due to sensitivity over the electric chair, resulting in obvious confusion. *The Kinematograph Weekly* (April 30) accurately pegged the picture as "High voltage melodrama mixing gangsterdom

Boris Karloff as the avenging angel John Ellman comforted by Nancy (Marguerite Churchill) in *The Walking Dead* (1936).

with the supernatural. The plot is, of course, frank Grand Guignol stuff ... and after finishing sustained suspense it ends on a lofty sentimental note, the echo of which sounds a moral." *Today's Cinema* (April 24) was less enthralled. "Quite obviously, much more might have been made of this 'beyond the veil' subject. As it stands, we have only to assess it in terms of straightforward melodrama and to remark that it is not singularly thrilling or exciting. Quite good popular entertainment." *The Walking Dead* was to be Boris Karloff's last American horror movie until *Son of Frankenstein* was released three years later.

The concept of government censorship had been batted around in Britain for several years; the issue was settled on April 30. The House of Commons announced there would be no government censorship—the present system would continue. When a member of Parliament Day asked if the present system was working, he received no answer (*Today's Cinema*, May 1).

By the month's end, local film censorship was again a hot issue. The Surrey Licensing Committee banned a film passed by the BBFC and classed another as "horrific." The Rev. H.C. Martin, vice chairman of the committee, felt both (unnamed) pictures were unfit for Surrey's "family type" cinemas. When asked why the picture was "horrific," Martin replied, "The hero was terrifying in appearance and the story developed into one of multiple murder" (*Today's Cinema*, May 28).

Revolt of the Zombies, from the producer of *White Zombie*, was trade shown on June 17 and dismissed two days later (*Today's Cinema*) as "Quite good fare for the masses. Adequate thrills and action. Quite interesting for the more unsophisticated type of patronage." Hopefully, the "unsophisticated patronage" enjoyed the picture—only two more horror movies would be available until 1939.

Dracula's Daughter (1936) was Universal's last horror movie produced under the Laemmle regime, before the British horror ban took effect. This brought the company's horror cycle, true to its name, back to the beginning with Dracula—at least in the picture's original treatment. Michael and John Brunas and Tom Weaver (*Universal Horrors*) revealed that scripter John L. Balderston had a *real* horror movie in mind, rather than the highly suggestive but relatively tame one that resulted. "I want to see [*Dracula's Daughter's*] loathsome deaf mute servants carry into her boudoir savage looking whips, chains, straps, etc., and hear the cries of the tortured victims" wrote Balderston in 1934. Incredibly, given *Dracula's* success, it took two *more* years to get the picture on the screen, and then in a considerably watered down form.

Bela Lugosi was, at one point, intended to appear. Although absent in the original treatment, he was later signed for $4,000, then dropped (but, fortunately for him, paid off). After finishing *The Mystery of the Mary Celeste* in England, he was reported by *The Kinematograph Weekly* to be "returning to Universal City to make *Dracula's Daughter*" and to "co-star with Karloff in two other productions for Universal this season—*Bluebeard* and *The Invisible Ray*."

The dropping of Lugosi and of Balderston's more lurid concepts indicates that Universal was feeling the heat generated both in the United States and the United Kingdom over horror movies. As directed by Lambert Hillyer, Garrett Fort's script was awash in *suggestion*.

After destroying Count Dracula, Dr. Von Helsing (Edward Van Sloan) is charged with murder. Sir Basil Humphrey (Gilbert Emery) of

Despite being suspected of being a lesbian, *Dracula's Daughter* (Gloria Holden) displays an unhealthy interest in Dr. Garth (Otto Kruger).

Scotland Yard thinks the doctor's tale of vampires is madness, and calls in psychiatrist Jeffrey Garth (Otto Kruger), Von Helsing's former student. Meanwhile, the Count's daughter Marya Zaleska (Gloria Holden) claims his corpse and, with the help of her servant Sandor (Irving Pichel), destroys it in the hope of exorcising her own vampirism. Her attempt at normalcy fails and, after meeting Garth at a party, she asks for his help. Despite her best effort, Zaleska loses control and attacks Lili (Nan Grey) after luring the girl into her apartment. Lili dies in a hospital. Suspecting the Countess, Garth goes to her and learns that she and Sandor have abducted Janet (Marguerite Churchill), his lover. Garth follows the trio to Transylvania with Sir Basil and Von Helsing at his heels. At Dracula's castle, she demands a trade—Garth's soul for Janet's—but she is killed with an arrow through her heart, fired by Sandor, who wanted to join her himself as an undead.

Sandor (Irving Pichel), jealous of the Countess' (Gloria Holden) interest in Dr. Garth (Otto Kruger) in *Dracula's Daughter* **(1936).**

The "old" Universal's last horror movie (until the "new" Universal's *Son of Frankenstein* [1939]) is often remembered today for its "implied lesbianism." The scene in question involves the vampiric seduction of Lili, the young street girl. After plying her with wine, the Countess "suggestively" suggests the girl remove some clothing—then, off camera, attacks. This is an ambiguous scene and it is doubtful that many 1936 viewers chose to see it as sexual.

Following *Dracula's Daughter*'s June 28 trade show, *Today's Cinema* (June 1) was dismissive. "Murky story of vampire's daughter ... ably handled in approved horrific vein ... facile revenge denouement. Not for juveniles; good booking of its type for adult masses." *Films and Filming* (June) was more blunt: "It's difficult to think that many people will be entertained by such a thoroughly morbid story. Designated by the

London County Council and other authorities as 'horrific,' this film is not for children."

In some ways, *Dracula's Daughter* seems to have been the proverbial last straw. Except in the extreme cases of *Frankenstein* and *Dr. Jekyll and Mr. Hyde*, the titles of horror movies under censorial scrutiny went unmentioned in the British press. Whether this was due to reticency on the part of the censors or the papers is not certain. Its purpose, though, was clear; naming the offending movie would pull patrons towards it like a magnet. This was certainly the case 20 years later when reviewers assaulted Hammer's *The Curse of Frankenstein*, and the picture broke attendance records. With *Dracula's Daughter*, the gloves came off, and the press, both trade and general, named names.

While *Dracula's Daughter* twisted on the critic's stake, false hope for three of Universal's superstars was announced. "Important developments concerning the Laemmles, father and son, in the production field–it has been decided to make a number of independent super productions produced by Jnr and backed by Snr," reported *Today's Cinema* (July 22). "One of the most important factors in the set up is the signing of James Whale, considered among the best of current directors." This intriguing premise never came to be; after Universal's *Show Boat* (1936), it was basically all over for all three. Carl Senior died in 1939; Junior went to MGM in May 1937, and resigned six months later. He died in 1979 without producing another film. James Whale directed eight more features with only *The Man in the Iron Mask* being much of a success.

"Horrifics" were the subject of an open letter to the BBFC in *Today's Cinema* on August 4. "Aren't you getting a little muddled?" the writer suggested. "One or two recent developments indicate that you are. Here is the question on 'horrific' films, for instance. Lord Tyrrell, at the recent C.E.A. Conference, said the category would be abolished because that sort of film had gone. It was a straightforward, unequivocal statement. Now comes the news that the London and Middlesex County Councils have decided that *The Walking Dead* is a 'horrific' film unsuitable for children, and the abolition of the 'horrific' category is to be deplored." Four days later, the dam burst.

Today's Cinema (August 8, 1936) led with the headline, "Horrific Film Category—Consultative Committee Will Reinstate It—Pressure on Film Censors—Protecting Children from Fright."

During the July meeting of the British Board of Film Censors, Chairman Lord Tyrell stated, "In view of the fact that the Board has always considered [horror] films to be unwholesome, the 'horrific' category has ceased to exist. The suggestion that there should be no such classification was no doubt well meant but it was never considered desirable by the Board. It is gratifying to find that those who advocated this innovation have come to the conclusion that it was wrong in principal and that the Board was correct in opposing the introduction of this third form of certificate (to accompany the 'A' and 'U')."

But, developments led local groups to insist that the "H" certificate be instituted. "It might be pointed out," said Sir Cecil Levita, chairman of the Consultative Committee, "that the authorities in Manchester have marked four films 'horrific,' and Surrey, Middlesex, and London have marked three as an immediate reply to the statement that the category has now gone. We are not squeamish and we take the big view; but we laid it down three years ago that if exhibitors want to show frightening films, they must warn the parents—if they don't, they will take the risk of losing their license." Levita added that the BBFC has no real power to deal with rating categories—the real power was held by the licensing authority.

"MGM's fantastic melodrama" *The Devil Doll* was trade shown on August 19 at the Adelphia and was praised in *Today's Cinema* (August 21) for its "amazing trick photography, good acting and suspense values. Excellent novelty booking for non-squeamish audiences."

The Devil Doll proved to be Tod Browning's swan song—only two features followed (*Miracles for Sale*, 1939, and *Inside Job*, 1946), and neither made an impact. The director who ushered in the horror cycle with *Dracula*, though, was at least there as it faded away.

Paul Lavond (Lionel Barrymore) is imprisoned on Devil's Island, framed by his unscrupulous banking partners. Along with Marcel (Henry B. Walthall) and his wife Malita (Rafaela Ottiano), Lavond escapes. Marcel is a scientist who has developed a method to miniaturize people, believing it will solve the world's overpopulation problems. But, after Marcel dies, Lavond takes Malita and the process to Paris, looking for revenge. Disguised as an old woman, Lavond uses the tiny terrors to rob his enemies and to force them to exonerate their master.

This was not quite what Browning and scripters Garrett Fort and Guy Endore envisioned when they were more or less "inspired" by Abraham Merritt's novel *Burn, Witch, Burn*. The trio saw the story, originally titled *The Witch of Timbuctoo*, as involving voodoo rather than pseudo-science. The use of witchcraft did not sit well with the production code administration but, even more worrisome, the script included suicide (*Dark Carnival* by David J. Skal and Elias Savada). More problems came from the BBFC which, after getting wind of the proposed voodoo angle, flatly said no. This made sense only in the senseless world of the BBFC, which seemingly had no difficulty with *White Zombie* or *Revolt of the Zombies*. At any rate, MGM caved in and replaced the occult with science fiction.

Fairly few horror movies were solid hits as the cycle wound down, due to several factors. Chief among them was public indifference. Pictures viewed as classics today made little financial impact during their release. For example, *Mark of the Vampire* earned $54,000 on an investment of $305,177, *Mad Love* lost $39,000, and *The Devil Doll* did $68,000. Based on these figures (from *Hollywood Cauldron* and *Dark Carnival*), making a horror movie in the mid-thirties didn't seem to be worth the trouble. By comparison, *Frankenstein* made a whopping $1 million. on an investment of $262,000.

On September 1, the BBFC restated a list of subjects that would put a film at risk of banning, which included: ministers of religion in equivocal situations, blasphemous incidents, objectional prison scenes, girls and women in states of intoxication, suggestive and indecorous dancing, nude and semi-nude figures, indecorum of dress and behavior, themes of habitual immorality, hanging, methods of crime open to imitation, murderous gang fighting, cruelty to animals, suggestive speech, and excessive drinking scenes. Incredibly, no mention was made of the "horrific."

Twickenham Studios bravely offered up Boris Karloff's *Juggernaut* for a trade show at the Piccadilly on September 8. While *definitely* not a horror movie, Karloff's presence as a doctor-murderer made it one to the public; this was *not* good timing. *Today's Cinema* (September 10) brushed off *Juggernaut* as a "medical melodrama. Strong meat for the masses. Regarded purely as melodramatic entertainment, one may overlook the narrative's occasional lack of conviction."

Gainsborough showed even more fortitude when *The Man Who Changed His Mind* (U.S. title—*The Man Who Lived Again*) was trade shown three days later. The "scientific melodrama" (*Today's Cinema*, September 14) was patronized as a "potent lure for the man in the street." The review didn't dwell on the picture's "horrific" content—the literal changing of human minds—but presented it as a "fantasy."

These two British made films were, unfortunately, planned before the bottom fell out of the demand for Karloff-type entertainment. One can only imagine their box office performances.

The BBFC answered the objections voiced by Sir Cecil Levita by issuing a brochure titled *Film Censorship Today*, containing the text of Lord Tyrell's presentation to the summer conference in July concerning horrifics. "Local licensing authorities," then stated Tyrell, "throughout the country declared that they were determined not to allow the exhibition of these films in the cinemas under their jurisdiction; and in view of the fact that the Board has always considered such films to be unwholesome, the 'horrific' has now ceased to exist." This viewpoint from July was then modified: "Nevertheless, the 'horrific' category remains, and will be used if it is found that any films are produced which come within its orbit. The suggestion that there should be this classification was no doubt well meant, but it was never considered desirable by the Board, although we gave way to the view that it should be inaugurated and given a trial. Those members of the trade who originally supported the proposal have since come to the conclusion that films of this nature are altogether undesirable and should not be made."

Based on the box office performances of *Mad Love*, *Mark of the Vampire*, and *The Devil Doll*, audiences had apparently come to the same conclusion.

However, not even the BBFC's strong stand and public indifference were enough for the Surrey County Council. On October 28, the Council took an unprecedented stance—it chose to act as its own censorial body to ban horror movies. *Today's Cinema* (October 29) reported that, "At the Surrey County Council meeting, the committee reported that it had considered the question of horrific films and was satisfied that not all films likely to frighten children were classed as horrific by the Board. It therefore recommended an amendment to the licensing regulation 23(a) to make it read: 'That no film which has been classified by the BBFC as "horrific" or, which, after inspection, is considered by the Council as likely to frighten or horrify children under the age of 16, shall be exhibited in the premises in any circumstances during the time that any child under, or appearing to be under, the age of 16 is therein.'"

The voice of reason (Tom Braddock, a council member) was then heard. Would, he asked, military pictures and newsreels of war be considered horrific since they could certainly frighten or horrify children? This aside, the scene was now set to protect British children from the dark.

"CHILDREN BANNED FROM 'HORRIFIC'" shouted the headline in *Today's Cinema* (November 2). "Adult Guardian Safeguard Not Sufficient. London CEA Approves."

This ruling, to take effect on January 1, 1937, would completely ban children under 16 from seeing a horror movie in London whether accompanied by a guardian or not. This not only encouraged cinema managers *not* to book horror films, but also encouraged Hollywood producers to stop producing them. Not that they needed much encouragement; the poor box office showing could not have been ignored. Trailers advertising horrifics, unless individually and specifically passed by the BBFC as "U," were also ruled not suitable for children.

The London County Council, the power behind the decision, recalled: "It has been the practice of the BBFC since January 1933, to class as 'horrific' any films which are likely to frighten or horrify children under the age of 16 years. On June 20, 1933, the Council amended No. 8 of its rules of management with regard to places of public entertainment to provide that when a film of this character is being shown at premises licensed by the Council—a special notice—THIS FILM IS UNSUITABLE FOR CHILDREN—be fixed to the Category Board."

This old ruling, at least in London, still placed considerable responsibility on parents. "The responsibility for allowing such children to see 'horrific' films is thus entirely one for their parents or guardians." Since these "horrifics" were classed as "A," they could be seen by children with parental consent, but how many parents took the trouble to preview the picture before giving that consent? The November 1 ruling took that problem out of parental hands.

"By 1935," the council added, "as the number of such films was increasing, we deemed it desirable to consider whether children should be permitted in any circumstance to see them even if accompanied by a parent or guardian."

At that time, in conjunction with the education committee and the Middlesex and Surrey councils, the LCC viewed "two typical horrifics— *The Invisible Man* and *Bride of Frankenstein*, which had been classed as such by the BBFC." Both had, naturally, been found to be "undesirable."

On June 24, 1936—following the release of *Dracula's Daughter*— Lord Tyrell had noted, rather confusingly, "Although I possess no personal experience of the matter, I am given to understand that the horrific film has gone." Since the Universal production ended shooting on March 10, and would not make another horror movie for over two years, *Lord* Tyrell's pronouncement was incredibly accurate. He added, on November 1, "Since January, 1933, 18 films have been classified as 'horrific' by the BBFC. In consequence of certain representations as to the character of two films which had *not* been classified as 'horrific,' we inspected them in July and decided to class them as 'horrific' as far as London is concerned. I don't think we shall see any more."

The board, joining forces with the Cinematograph Exhibitors' Association and the education committee, now presented a united front, recommending: "That, as from, and including January 1, 1937, no cinematograph film which is classed by the British Board of Film Censors as 'horrific' shall be exhibited at the premises during any time that any child under the age of 16 years is therein."

On November 4, two days after this statement was issued, Warner Bros.' fantasy, *The Walking Dead*, featuring one of Boris Karloff's most sensitive performances, was classed as horrific by the London County Council. The BBFC had passed it as "A," but "the LCC arranged to view the film to decide whether it should be regarded as 'horrific,'" *The Cinema* reported. The Surrey County Council had already pronounced the picture to be "horrific." A month later, *The Cinema* (December 2, 1936) reported that the Surrey County Council had classed three more (unnamed) pictures as "horrific."

As 1936 wound down, the first "horror cycle" died with it. Hollywood's infatuation with the genre—a full blown romance four years earlier—was over. Nothing remotely resembling a horror movie would slither from its studios in 1937 or 1938. Those films already produced that had not yet reached British cinemas would have severe difficulties being exhibited. Why should a cinema manager book a picture from which children would be banned? Parents, looking for a night at the movies with their children, were not looking for a horrific picture. And, if they were, they were going to have a long wait.

1937—Banned in Britain

Even though Hollywood had shut down its production of horror movies, their effect was still being felt in Britain, where censors and local watch groups were determined to make this hiatus permanent. On January 1, children were banned from two unnamed "A"-rated horrifics playing in Birmingham. The "H" "advisory" was firmly in effect, but the BBFC would be hard put to find any new pictures worthy of the classification.

In 1936, 763 feature films had been trade shown in London—57 more than in the previous year. Of these pictures, only four were rated as fantasy; with Great Britain and the United States each producing two. Mystery melodramas numbered 36, with Britain supplying only six. Horror movies were, significantly, not given a separate category.

Horror movies were very much on the minds of the Essex County Council, though. *The Kinematograph Weekly* (January 7) headlined "Horrific Ban in Essex—New Regulation Enforced." What had been promised for over a year was finally a reality: "A new ban imposed by the Essex County Council forbids the admission of children under 16 to see 'horror' films not passed for universal admission in any circumstances. Trailers are also banned." In effect, adults who wanted to see a horror movie with their children were also banned, since parental accompaniment was no longer part of the mix.

The Licensing Committee declared that, due to previous rulings, all horror films were given an "A" classification, meaning that they "cannot be seen by children under 16 unless accompanied by a parent or adult guardian. Thus, at present, the responsibility for allowing children to see 'horror' films rested entirely with their parents or guardians; and, as there might be a likelihood of the number of such films increasing, the Committee had decided that children should not be permitted to see 'horror' films in Essex under any circumstances." However, by early 1937, this was clearly not the case; there *was* no "likelihood of the number of such films increasing."

Today's Cinema (January 6) added, "When the cinematograph film classed as a 'horror' film is included in the current programme of films to be exhibited at the premises the licensee shall affix a notice in block letters (not less than 1½ inches) in the following terms: 'Children under 16 not admitted to this film.'"

This concern about children's film viewing had great financial implications. The market was judged as being worth £1,000,000. At a conference held late in 1936, almost 100 authorities on children's behavior and social organizations convened. The film industry had no representatives, even though a fortune was at stake. The major point made was if the highly impressionable minds of children could be harmed by motion pictures, then every effort should be made to protect them.

It was judged that there were almost six million British children between the ages of 5 and 15 and that many of them attended cinemas fairly regularly. The "ideal children's programme" was felt to consist of a two reel comedy, a cartoon, a simplistic feature (no longer than an hour) containing an admirable hero and little dialogue, and a serial episode. There were also those who supported the inclusion of edited down "A" features of the "non horrific" kind.

On January 11, Alderman H.H. Heather, a former teacher and current chairman of the Essex Committee of Licensing of Places of Public Entertainment, upheld the new regulation. He further suggested that all previous standards used for "horrifics" be repealed and replaced by more stringent measures. Other localities quickly followed, and it was now suicidal for a cinema manager to book a horror movie.

An even stranger (and totally absurd) position was taken by F.E. Harrison, director of education in Blackpool. Harrison felt that *all* school age children should be banned from *all* movies without a note of permission from their head teacher! "I feel," he said (*Today's Cinema*, January 7), "that it would save a lot of children. Pictures, with children, are becoming a religion. Attending the pictures today is more of a fetish than the attendance of our grandfathers at church. It is becoming a positive curse, a menace to the child." Three weeks later, Harry Day, representing Scotland, addressed the House of Commons on the issue of

Boris Karloff takes a pre-ban break from horror, shown running his lines with Warner Oland in *Charlie Chan of the Opera* **(1936).**

"objectionable pictures which are harmful to the minds of children" (*Kinematograph Weekly*, January 28).

A brief reality check took place at a debate of the Southampton Council concerning underage children sneaking into "horrifics," with the tacit consent of cinema managers. Alderman Mouland ventured, "I do not think any cinema manager would run the risk of breaking the regulation."

"Oh, don't be silly!" countered Alderman Lewis (*Today's Cinema*, January 28).

As the debate over horror continued to rage, Boris Karloff slipped quietly into London in *Charlie Chan at the Opera* ("A Battle of Wits— Chan vs. Karloff") and *Juggernaut* ("The Screen's Greatest Monster"). Neither picture showcased Karloff in his specialty.

Perhaps the most ludicrous position of all was taken by an Irish judge on February 16: he felt that *all* children should be banned unilaterally from *all* movies!

In a February 24 editorial, *Today's Cinema* looked squarely at the situation. "The children of today are no worse or better than they were 50 or 100 years ago. The parents of the children are their best guardians and teachers of common sense and morals. Now—what does all this 'children and films' really amount to?"

It amounted, basically, to sex, crime, and horror. The paper felt that children do not become sexually awake until they are *no longer* children, and that "sex scenes" in movies bored them. As to crime, "some of the uplifters seem to think that because a boy runs around with a popgun, he is on the high road to becoming a gangster." Concerning horror movies, the writer felt the situation was under complete control. "Of course, horror films are not the things for children. But exhibitors have already discovered that: exhibitors are unanimous in approving and accepting the regulations which prevent children from seeing horror films. So—what's all the fuss about?"

However, it must be pointed out that several Mickey Mouse cartoons were judged to be horrific! At the Bath Children's Cinema Council, a survey of 1,553 children revealed that half of them found incidents involving Disney's rodent terrifying. Oliver Bell, speaking for the British Film Institute, said, "The adult may be amused, but the child would fear that the abnormal physical experiences depicted might happen to itself."

The National Council for Women, at its March meeting, joined the fray. "I have been told," said Mrs. A. Munro MacRobert, "of a boy of nine who fell unconscious in a cinema and screamed all night after witnessing an on screen murder." As to the "H" certificate, she felt that "U" pictures are "often just as detrimental to the young mind" (*Today's Cinema*, March 23).

All this seems redundant, though, as the *Kinematograph Weekly* (March 18) headlined "PRODUCERS ABANDON THE HOR-RIFIC—Needless Alarm of Public Bodies." The paper felt the question of horror movies was a moot one. "The vogue of such films is at an end."

At the March 6 session of Parliament, G.M. Garro-Jones (Labour MP) asked the Home Office secretary whether he was aware of the debate over "horrifics," which he categorized as "films that healthy people have a natural repugnance for." It was noted that, since 1932, only 18 films had been judged as horrific. Also mentioned was Lord Tyrell's summer of 1936 pronouncement that "this class of subject would not be produced in the future, having regard to the difficulty which the trade had experienced in the renting of such films."

Concerning the powers held by local watch groups, it was pointed out that many—no matter whether the picture had been certified by the BBFC—refused to allow the film to be shown. Now that the "H" classification was generally in use, there was little use for it. "It would seem that for all practical purposes," said Sir John Simon, the Home secretary, "there is little likelihood of films of this character being made, especially as exhibitors have expressed themselves that such films are not required. In view of the cessation of such films in the horrific group, such certification would hardly appear necessary. As if on cue, Joseph I. Breen, director of the Production Code Administration ("the man who makes films safe for families"), arrived in London on April 1. He assured his hosts that, "[t]he greatest care is being taken to ensure that nothing in Hollywood is produced that could offend British sensibilities."

Then, one of the most inexplicable incidents in this series of them occurred. The "H" classification had previously been an advisory; cinema managers were responsible for displaying it as a warning to parents. The action taken as of January 1, 1937, was a defensive move by the BBFC to appease the local watch groups, but was basically pointless due to the curtailed production of the pictures to which it referred. But, on April 23, the London County Council requested that the "H" be instituted as an *official* category, joining "U" and "A" as an equal partner. The horror movie was dead, but the LCC wanted it buried.

Meanwhile, Boris Karloff flickered across a trade show screen in *Night Key*, a thrill-less "thriller" in which the former king of former horror movies appeared for Universal, its former champion. This was Karloff's first picture for Universal since 1936's *The Invisible Ray*; his services would not be required again by the studio he enriched until 1939's *Son of Frankenstein*.

Karloff was able to weather the drought caused by horror's loss of fashion through a contract with Warner Bros. he luckily signed before the genre collapsed. This resulted in a mediocre trio consisting of *West of Shanghai*, *The Invisible Menace*, and *Devil's Island*, which at least tided him over until horror movies made their comeback. *Devil's Island* was denied a BBFC certificate as to not offend the French.

Bela Lugosi was not as fortunate. After fulfilling his contract with Universal in *Postal Inspector*, filmed in June 1936, his career hit rock bottom; he appeared on only two serials from then until *Son of Frankenstein*'s January 1939 release. "The mortgage company got my house," he confessed in a 1942 interview with Frederick C. Othman (in Arthur Lening's *The Count*). "I sold one car, then the other. I borrowed where I could, but who considered a jobless spook a good risk? By the end of 1937, I was at my wit's end. I was forced to go on relief."

On June 7, the London County Council got its wish when *The Thirteenth Chair*, an MGM thriller, was trade shown in London and slapped with an "H" certificate. Why this innocuous picture became the first to receive the "H" is not certain; it was probably done as an appeasement to the watchdogs and as a warning to Hollywood. An earlier movie of Bayard Veiller's play was filmed in 1929 with Bela Lugosi.

Inspector Marney (Lewis Stone) arrives in Calcutta to investigate the stabbing death of Leonard Leith, whose body has been cremated. John Wales (Henry Daniell) warns Marney to go lightly due to Leith's government connections. He suggests that Rosalie La Grange (Dame May Whitty), a local medium, conduct a séance to discover the murderer's identity. Invited are the "usual suspects," including Helen (Elissa Landi) and Lionel Trent (Ralph Forbes), Dr. Mason (Charles Trowbridge), the governor (Holmes Herbert), and lovers Nell O'Neill (Madge Evans) and Dick Crosby (Thomas Beck), the governor's son. Thirteen people are seated around the table, and Wales is stabbed by one of them during the séance.

Madame La Grange is revealed to be Nell's mother when the latter becomes the prime suspect—she was seated next to Wales during the séance. To protect her daughter, La Grange develops a grotesque scheme. A second séance is held—with Wales' corpse in the murder chair. When the lights go on, his arm is raised, pointing to the missing knife, which is stuck in the ceiling. In the following confusion, Dr. Mason (whose wife Leith stole) confesses to both murders. Fearing that Wales was on to him, Mason killed him.

The picture is fairly creepy in its stagebound way, and a bit more so when Nell disgustedly takes Wales' dead hand during the séance, but there is really nothing here to warrant an "H."

"*The Thirteenth Chair*," said *Today's Cinema* (June 9), "is the first film to be given an 'H' certificate, but we are of the opinion that the usual adult certificate would have suited it equally as well." Incredibly, *Night Must Fall*, with a psycho (Robert Montgomery) running around with a severed head in a hat box, was trade shown a few days later as an "A." *Today's Cinema* (June 12) commented on the picture's sense of "creeping horror" and its "terrifying climax."

On June 24, the BBFC revealed that of the 2,415 pictures screened in 1936, 2,000 were rated "U," 413 rated "A," and only 2 were given the

"H" *advisory*. Why the new "H" *certificate* was felt to be necessary will remain a mystery. With no live-action movies to certify as horrific, the BBFC now turned its attention to cartoons. "Some are definitely unsuitable for children," reported *The Kinematograph Weekly* (July 15), "and great care should be exercised to avoid any which might frighten or supply content for nightmare."

1938—Signs of Life

Boris Karloff, the former "king" of the former horror genre, seemed less regal on January 5, 1938, when Warner Bros.' *The Invisible Menace* opened. Adapted from a Broadway play by Ralph Spencer Zink, this misleadingly titled non-thriller cast Karloff as a stereotyped red herring character involved in a murder case at an Army base. "Although it is in no sense a macabre and spine chilling picture," said *Today's Cinema*, "it is very strong indeed in thrilling and somewhat suspenseful action. Narration adheres to beaten track of species, focusing heavy suspicion on an innocent man. Dependable offering for the masses."

The same day, Bette Davis and Humphrey Bogart were deemed unacceptable for children in *Marked Woman*, a typical Warner Bros. gangster melodrama of the period. The Smethwick Watch Committee banned "any child under, or appearing to be under, the age of 16 years." The year got off to a poor start and soon got worse.

The BBFC was approached, on May 4, by the National Council of Women, to closely scrutinize cartoons and shorts. "Characters shown may frighten small children," it was reported in *The Kinematograph Weekly*. "These cartoons should be classed as unsuitable for children under 12. Children at matinees where cartoons were shown containing terrifying characters sometimes became quite hysterical with terror."

Britain had a *real* horror movie on its hands in director Abel Gance's *J'Accuse!*, a sound version of his controversial silent anti-war tract. Although the picture *did* contain truly horrific images of mutilated soldiers rising from their graves to protest the inhumanity of war, the aim of the film was certainly higher than a *Frankenstein* movie and certainly did not deserve to be placed in the same class. *J'Accuse!* pointed out the weakness of the "H" certificate (or, perhaps, *any* film classification method) in that it *defied* classification.

Jean Diaz (Victor Francen), the sole survivor of a massacre prior to the end of World War I, is horrified by the growing move toward rearmament and the threat of another war. He returns to the graves of the war dead and implores them to rise and confront the living who would cause more destruction. Recently made available on video, *J'Accuse!* remains an emotional experience, and despite quantum leaps in cinema technology, its horrors remain difficult to watch despite the dated presentation.

Today's Cinema (May 4) exposed the picture's importance and the need for its exhibition. "Dedicated to the 'dead of the next war,' this magnificent French film has been given an 'H' certificate and must not be shown to those under 16. It should be seen by everybody over 16; for it is probably the most terrific indictment against war that the screen has ever seen. At a moment when all the 'civilized' nations of the world are feverishly rearming it could not have been more timely." Important message aside, the BBFC saw fit to sink the picture with an "H" due to the horrific makeups. "This resurrection sequence," added *Today's Cinema*, "is emotionally one of the most powerful in the film. It does not even shirk glimpses at the hideously disfigured appearance of men who have died of face wounds. Directed with fine integrity as a passionate anti-war indictment, it has an unrelieved note of tragedy throughout."

The London County Council had to deal with more traditional themes when reissues of earlier horror movies were announced. Since these pictures were made *before* the "H" certificate joined the "A" and "U" on equal footing, potential problems loomed. The LCC felt that notice should be placed at all cinemas exhibiting a picture originally recognized as "horrific," but passed as an "A." "Particular attention is drawn to the regulations that children up to 16 years of age must not be present during the exhibition of an 'A' film unless accompanied by a parent or other adult who is for the time being in bona-fide charge of such children." A particular case in point was *Frankenstein*.

The monster that incensed censors and watch groups six years ago was again on the rampage, receiving a London trade showing on July 13. *Frankenstein*'s release was "not fixed," but its certificate was "A." *Today's Cinema* (July 15) reminded its readers that *Frankenstein* had previously been reviewed on January 21, 1932, but failed to mention the furor the picture had caused. "In its day, *Frankenstein* was almost a household term of reference for the horror film, and even now its macabre thrill and sensation should make patrons sit up in their seats. Narration remains unsurpassed in sheer horror, thrill, and macabre incident."

This mid–July trade show is interesting when compared to events in Los Angeles three weeks later. *The Hollywood Reporter* (August 6) headlined "THREE HORROR PIX FOR 30¢ FILLS LOCAL THE-ATRE TO CAPACITY 21 HRS A DAY." The three "pix" were *Dracula*, *Frankenstein*, and *Son of Kong*, and the theatre was the Regina in Wilshire: "We defy you to stand for this much horror in one show." The *Reporter* said that "Attempts to insert cartoons between two of the features were met with hisses."

Horror-hungry patrons (supposedly) came from as far as Stockton, Fresno, and San Diego. Greg Mank (*It's Alive!*) reported that "Lines formed around the Regina until well past midnight, and Universal, hearing of the sell-out business, rushed out *Dracula* and *Frankenstein* on a double bill." This has been the accepted version and may well be the case, but one must wonder about the role played by the earlier London trade show.

Frankenstein and *Dracula* were eventually reissued in Britain in December through General Film Distributors. "We Dare You to Book These Two Pictures and Show Them on One Programme!" screamed a trade ad; the Rialto, on Coventry Street, packed in 30,811 brave souls in the first five weeks.

Due to the successful runs at the Regina and, later, at the Rialto, it seems as though horror was back. Universal evidently thought so, announcing in *The Hollywood Reporter* (September 21) its plans to remake *The Raven* with Karloff and Lugosi. "The studio has a fresh angle for the new version," stated the *Reporter*. Fortunately, this poor idea was scrapped, and replaced with a better one. Universal added Basil Rathbone and Lionel Atwill to the mix and began *Son of Frankenstein* on October 17.

British censors and watchdogs, holding the "H" certificate like a crucifix, had little to fear if the genre returned, since the under 16 set was now protected. The horror movies that they had fought to suppress refused to go away for one simple reason: people enjoyed them. Now that Hollywood was convinced that their termination had been a mistake, it was time for a second cycle to begin. Many in Britain may not have liked the return of horrifics, but as the events warned about in *J'Accuse!* moved closer to reality, more serious matters were at hand. As *Son of Frankenstein* was playing in British cinemas, Europe was moving towards war. By the time a British-made horror movie (*Dark Eyes of London*) was in release, World War II was three months old.

1939—Back
from the Dead

Of 732 features trade shown in Britain in 1938, *Today's Cinema* (January 4) categorized none, either made in the United States or the United Kingdom, as fantasy. One hundred fifteen, however, were classed as "mystery melodrama," 93 of which were made in the United States. The next day, *horror* flapped its way back on the wings of *The Vampire Bat* when the 1932 picture was reissued by, oddly enough, Exclusive. The company would later, as Hammer Film Productions, evoke *The Curse of Frankenstein* (1957) and usher in an era of screen horror undreamed of in the thirties.

Again proving the pointlessness of the *new* "H" (which had been used only twice in the previous two years), *They Drive by Night* was trade shown as an "A" on January 6. While not strictly a "horror movie," this British film contained scenes more frightening than anything in the "H" certified *The Thirteenth Chair*.

Shorty Matthews (Emlyn Williams), released from a short prison term, returns to his old haunts and looks up Alice, an old girlfriend, now a dance "hostess." He finds her dead—strangled with a silk stocking. He is now a suspect and on the run. Shorty meets Wally (Allan Jeayes), who gives him a lift to London. Wally, suspicious of Shorty, threatens to take him to the police; they skid, and Shorty replaces the injured driver at the wheel. Stopping at a café, Shorty saves Molly (Anna Konstam) from a sexual assault, and she joins forces with him. In London, she hides him in an empty house and, at a dance hall, looks for men who patronized Alice. She meets Hoover (Ernest Thesiger), a "student of psychology,"

151

Basil Rathbone and Boris Karloff appear off the set with *Son of Frankenstein*'s (1939) *real* horror, Donnie Dunagan.

who offers his services. At his home which is filled with sex crime books, Molly finds a drawer filled with silk stockings. When Hoover assaults her, Shorty bursts in and subdues the maniac.

Today's Cinema (January 7) praised the "lurid story" and "grisly climax," and called the picture "exciting entertainment." Thesiger, who played *The Old Dark House* and *Bride of Frankenstein* for laughs, is in earnest here, creating one of the decade's most perverted screen psychotics. Compared to this one, *The Thirteenth Chair* deserved a "U."

A month later, at a meeting of the Belfast Corporation, the attempted reversal of the banning of *Frankenstein* was unsuccessful. With *Son of Frankenstein*'s trade show less than two weeks away, the ban was yet another absurd action by local watchdogs.

Benson (Edgar Norton) menaced by the monster (Boris Karloff) as both the character and the horror genre return to life in *Son of Frankenstein* (1939).

The Deal Council denied horror movies a valentine on February 14 by copying the London County Council's position on the "H," retroactive to January 1. Local exhibitors were to be notified that any pictures classed as "horrific" by the LCC must be given a similar classification. The next day, the first *true* horror movie since 1936 was announced in the trades; the LCC would finally have a realistic use for the "H."

"General Film Distributors new trade show line-up is headed by the eagerly anticipated new Universal super shocker *Son of Frankenstein*," head-lined *Today's Cinema* (February 15). "Universal Pictures, the famed producers of the screen's most notable all time shockers, should crown all former 'horror' achievements."

However, adult filmgoers planning to take their infants to *Son of Frankenstein* were in for an additional shock: the Southampton Borough Council, on February 15, banned "babies in arms" from "H" certified pictures! Alderman Mouland, chairman, said, "The London Authority and other bodies adopted new regulations concerning these films, and the Committee recommended the adoption of the following clause for Southampton: 'any child (*whether in arms or not*)' shall be excluded."

As the February 16th trade show at the Cambridge approached, London was covered with *Son of Frankenstein* posters: "The Dead Live and the Living Die in a Film That Reaches New Heights of Horror" ... "The Menace of Rathbone!"..."The Fright of Karloff."..."The Horror of Lugosi."..."The Hate of Atwill." Release was scheduled for May 15. *Today's Cinema* (February 18) was impressed with Hollywood's return to horror, almost as if it had never gone away. "With the memory of the original Frankenstein horrors still with them—stimulated, no doubt, by the recent successful reissue—a huge public awaits these frankly frightening further exploits. The narration is out for the sheer thrill, and abundantly delivers the goods. Horrific highlights include the repellently fascinating incident of monster brought back to life ... a couple of cold blooded murders ... and a gruesome climax. Arresting novelty with big exploitation angles." If nothing else, *Son of Frankenstein* validated the "H" certificate.

On March 16, Karloff returned to his native soil in *another* horrific—albeit one three years old—when the Warner Bros. reissue *The Walking Dead* was trade shown. Oddly, the picture was shown with the following proviso: London and Middlesex certified it as "H," while the rest of the UK, presumably, could exhibit it as "A."

On May 4, the fourth *new* picture to receive the "H" was trade shown: the provocatively titled *Boy Slaves*. This minor RKO production did not concern, as its title suggests, the sexual molestation of children. Its slim plot explored juvenile delinquents sentenced to a labor camp. "The sordid detail depicted in this picture," sniffed *Today's Cinema* (May 5) "fortunately has no parallel in this country. One is not prepared to say that the film merits a horror certificate, for much of the incident deals with mere stupid cruelty ... their beating up by bosses, their putrid food. Certainly the callous victimization of young boys does not appear to represent entertainment in the accepted sense of the word." *Variety* merely blew it off as "filler for the duals," exhibiting, perhaps, a stronger stomach.

As the horror movie slowly returned to life, British cinema owners were justifiably confused as to how and to whom the pictures should be

Horror returns to stay in *Son of Frankenstein* (1939).

exhibited. The East Ham Corporation, for example, noting that "there will be several releases in the near future of films with the category of 'horrific'," requested that the Home Counties Licensing Authority "incorporate a clause in next year's license so that exhibitors will know where they stand."

Several odd recipients of the "H" followed in quiet succession. *The Gorilla*, featuring the Ritz Brothers and Bela Lugosi, was the third film version (following those of 1927 and 1931) of Ralph Spence's play, with an emphasis split between smiles and suspense. Despite the presence of a supposed "killer gorilla" and Bela Lugosi ("so sinister that he cannot possibly be guilty" opined *Today's Cinema*), this is more comedy than thriller.

On Borrowed Time, a gentle, sentimental fantasy, was incredibly branded with the dread "H." Gramps Northrup (Lionel Barrymore) keeps Death, calling himself Mr. Brink (Cedric Hardwicke), at bay by trapping him in an apple tree to the delight of his grandson Pud (Bobs Watson). *Today's Cinema* (August 4) felt that the picture was unsuitable for children, "in that they will not comprehend it, but we are amazed that it should be shackled by a 'horrific' certificate."

Next in line was *Hell's Kitchen*, featuring the Dead End Kids and Ronald Reagan, chronicling the victimization of a pack of delinquents at a "boys' home." While the picture may not have been suitable for children (or anyone), it was certainly *not* horrific and served to point out the inadequacy of the "H" certificate.

Bob Hope was the next to taste the "H" in *The Cat and the Canary* which, like *The Gorilla*, mixed laughs and chills but contained far more of both. "It has an 'H' certificate and deserves it," announced *Today's Cinema* (October 3), which chose to downplay the film's basically comedic approach. While there are several frightening scenes, the picture depends more on Hope's quips than quakes, making it an arguable "H" recipient. "This sort of thing is often done—and often badly," the paper accurately noted. "Here it is all done well."

The Cat and the Canary was the eighth picture to receive the "H" certificate, and *Today's Cinema* (August 8) offered an insightful look into its machinations. "The world will never be satisfied with censorship. Its ways and decisions are too difficult to understand. In the film industry, the problem has been complicated by the introduction of a third certificate. This, instead of simplifying the task of classification, has served to make it far more difficult. It has now fallen on the censors to define what is horror: a task on which we seriously advised them to call in the help of a psychologist, lest they fall too frequently into absurdity."

The writer cannily observed that horror can only be created by a film if its audience has the mental ability to allow itself to be horrified, and questioned whether the censors truly understood what horrified children, for whose protection the "H" was created. "Beauty is in the eye of the beholder and the same is true of horror. The real problem for the censors is to find out what it is that horrifies children before attempting to classify it under categories."

Birth of a Baby, of all things, next incurred the "H," but the Surrey Council complicated matters on August 16 by instituting a new local certificate. The picture was exhibited under an "E," for Educational. When Karloff's *The Man They Could Not Hang* was trade shown on October 16, it was unrated with an unfixed release date. It later, naturally, was certified "H."

Dark Eyes of London (U.S. title—*The Human Monster*) was a groundbreaker; it was the first British-made picture to receive the "H" certificate. The film provided Bela Lugosi with one of the few decent acting opportunities made available to him after the comeback of horror, and he made the most of it.

Inspector Holt (Hugh Williams) of Scotland Yard is investigating five deaths by drowning—all victims were insured through an insurance company operated by Dr. Orloff (Bela Lugosi). Orloff is also a philanthropist who supports the Home for the Destitute Blind in Greenwich. The home is operated by Mr. Dearborn, a kindly blind man who reads to his charges from a Braille Bible, aided by Jake (Wilfred Walter), his deformed, blind assistant. Stewart (Gerald Pring), who owes Orloff money, fulfills his promise to visit the home and meets Dr. Orloff (Dearborn is "out") and has a Braille note secreted into his pocket by Lew (Arthur E. Owen), a blind violinist. Moments later, Stewart is murdered by Jake. Stewart's body is fished out of the Thames, an apparent drowning victim like the rest, but his lungs contain tap water. Grogan (Alexander Field), a small-time forger, is taken in by Orloff, who threatens him into signing Stewart's insurance policy, with the doctor as the beneficiary. When Holt learns of this, Orloff explains that it was done as part of the loan agreement. Grogan is quickly killed by Jake, and Stewart's daughter Diana (Greta Gynt) is hired by Orloff to be Dearborn's secretary. Dr. Orloff has since learned about the note and deals with Lew harshly—he destroys his hearing. Holt has deduced that Dr. Orloff is behind the killings, and so has Diana. Orloff puts Jake on her trail, but the police frighten him away. Holt tells Dearborn that the doctor has been supporting the institute only to take advantage of the blind. Diana later dis-

Dr. Orloff (Bela Lugosi), revealing his true nature to Diane Stewart (Greta Gynt) in *The Dark Eyes of London* (1939), Britain's first "H" certificate production (*courtesy of Randy Vest*).

covers that Dearborn is not blind; and worse, he is actually Dr. Orloff in disguise! He binds her, then drowns Lew to finally silence him. Orloff orders Jake to murder Diana, but he kills the doctor instead when he realizes what Orloff did to Lew, his only friend.

"This adaptation of one of Edgar Wallace's best known thrillers has an 'H' certificate—and deserves it," opined *Today's Cinema* (October 20). The producer also *sought* it; the original story lacked the picture's horror touches, added to cash in on the genre's return. Most of the obvious horrific content came courtesy of the grotesque Jake, but more subtle and upsetting was the victimization of the blind. Bryan Senn (*Cult Movies*) accurately described *Dark Eyes of London* as a "crime drama dressed up as a horror picture for the benefit of its star. These elements aside, the film retains the crime-thriller structure, and, as such, the viewer must wade through scene after scene of detectives at work."

Jake (Wilfred Walter), shot by Dr. Orloff (Bela Lugosi), his unappreciative boss, in *Dark Eyes of London* (1939), Britain's first entry in horror's second wave (*courtesy of Randy Vest*).

Dark Eyes of London was also the last true British-made horror film to receive the "H" certificate. Due to the real horror of World War II (1939–1945), filmmakers in the UK wisely avoided their production. The "H" certificate was replaced on January 1, 1951, by the "X," which covered, like a wet blanket, all manners of "objectional" material from sleazy sex to harmless horror.

Humphrey Bogart, in this pre–*Maltese Falcon* period, had balked at the pictures being handed him at Warner Bros. Supposedly to keep him in line, Bogey was cast as a pseudo-vampire in *The Return of Dr. X*, in which he sported a hairstyle reminding one of the *Bride of Frankenstein* with its silver streak. His Dr. X was described by *Today's Cinema* (November 15) as "suitably repellent." This mediocre picture was the last of the decade to receive the "H" certificate.

Due to the war, lesser American pictures had difficulty being shown in the UK, and many horror movies went unseen until the hostilities ended. Those horror pictures receiving the "H" during the forties were: *The Monster and the Girl* (1941), *The Ghost of Frankenstein* (1942), *The Invisible Man's Revenge, Return of the Vampire* (1945), *The Mad Ghoul, The Lady and the Monster, Frankenstein Meets the Wolfman, The Ape Man, Voodoo Man, The Corpse Vanishes, The Mummy's Curse, House of Franken-stein, The Mysterious Doctor, The Vampire's Ghost, Jungle Captive* (all 1946), *The Mummy's Ghost, The Mummy's Tomb* (1947), *House of Dracula, Fall of the House of Usher, Dead Men Walk, The Monster Maker, Tall, Dark, and Gruesome* (all 1948), and *Captive Wild Women* (1950). *Bedlam* (1946), concerning mistreatment of the mentally ill, was banned.

The last word on the "H" certificate for 1939 was sounded in December when the Margate Town Council banned all movies bearing that certificate for 1940. But, the laugh was on them; there *were* none.

Afterword

by Gregory William Mank

It was Macabre-in-Excelsis.

It was the Golden Age of Hollywood Horror—a crazy, madly creative, artistically daring era where a 500-year old vampire inspired passionate fan mail, a 3,700-year-old mummy became the screen's most ardent lover, and a monster made from desecrated corpses had the most beautiful soul of all.

Hamlet had told the players to "hold the mirror up to nature." But the mirror that such directors as James Whale and Tod Browning held up in these amok Hollywood fairy tales was a wicked funhouse mirror—and the reflections that Boris Karloff and Bela Lugosi and Lionel Atwill tossed back were baroque distortions of sex, religion, and the concept of humanity itself.

The censors had plenty to ogle.

Dracula, Universal, 1931. Bela Lugosi's Vampire King is the Devil himself—offering his candlelit "I bid you welcome!" glamorous as mortal sin as he wears the cape in which Lugosi himself was destined to be buried. As we enter the hell of his Transylvania castle, wolves howl in the night, three vampire beauties lurk in the shadows, and "we" are Dwight Frye's Renfield—fated by the film's trickery to become a fly-and-spider gobbling lunatic by the second act. As David J. Skal wrote of the first ten minutes of Tod Browning's *Dracula* in his book *Hollywood Gothic*:

> The high gothic architecture is unmistakably ecclesiastical—
> Castle Dracula is religion in ruins.... An unholy trinity of bats is

161

observed. ...There is talk of wine and blood. ...Three silent women who approach are banished, and a male-to-male blood ritual is performed.

Frankenstein, Universal, 1931. Colin Clive, an alcoholic, tormented actor, his young, cadaverous face perfect for some sculptor creating a likeness of Christ on the cross, is our "God" here; "It's Alive!" he apocalyptically screams over the moving hand of Karloff's Monster—man-made, sewn together from corpses, and one of the most beloved icons of the cinema. As the Monster plays with Little Maria by the mountain lake, he is the bogeyman of our childhood nightmares, come to play with us, and laugh with us, and—finally—to drown us; in a bitter irony (and restored footage), the deed horrifies the poor Monster himself. As Phil Hardy wrote of James Whale's *Frankenstein* in *The Encyclopedia of Horror Movies*:

> Illuminated by Karloff's performance, the film has a weird, fairytale beauty. ...But its importance lies in the fact that its Monster is put forward at least ambivalently as hero, inducing a note of discreet but profound eroticism to the genre as well as an indication that it was perfectly capable of challenging—even undermining—social conventions.

And undermine and challenge them they did, as the Big Horror Films just kept-a-coming: *Dr. Jekyll and Mr. Hyde* (Paramount, 1931), with Fredric March's Oscar-winning, ape-like Hyde gleefully sexually tormenting Miriam Hopkins; *The Mummy* (Universal, 1932), with Karloff ardently chasing the soul of his beloved Anck-es-en-Amon across the centuries; *King Kong*, with Skull Island's giant ape titillating Depression audiences as he rampaged through New York City—and winning all their sympathy with his last-ditch stand atop the Empire State Building.

Early 1930s Hollywood was sensational in its tone, almost *circus maxiumus* in its style; the top stars of the 1930s were exotics, such as Garbo ("La Divina") and Jean Harlow ("The Platinum Blonde Bomb-shell"). The horror stars were among the most exotic of all.

KARLOFF, as Universal proclaimed him for much of the early/mid–1930s; gaunt, sensitive, devilishly handsome, with remarkably deep brown eyes ("You could *drown* in them!" gushed Frances Drake, his co-star of *The Invisible Ray*, 50 years later); a British exile, destined to charm leading ladies and interviewers ("I have just met the most amazing man in Hollywood," rhapsodized fan magazine writer Mary Sharon in the early 1930s. "I like Boris Karloff. Tremendously.") A super actor, full of quirky insights and love for his "dear old Monster": "It was as though man, in his blundering, searching attempts to improve himself, was to find himself deserted by his God."

Bela Lugosi, demonically attractive, a blue-eyed former Romeo of the classical stage in Hungary, with sex appeal ("He was incredible—the sexiest man I ever knew!" sighed Carroll Borland, Bela's "Luna" of *Mark of the Vampire*); he inspired purple prose in fan magazine writers (e.g., Gladys Hall in 1929; "He has touched the charnel houses of the Pluton-ian shores. He has ripped the heart of the night from its most foul hid-ing place.") An irreplaceable personality, destined to Hollywood tragedy, bequeathing an Oscar-winning role for Martin Landau in *Ed Wood* (1994), his blessing and his curse was his passion: "Women wrote me letters! Ah, what letters women wrote me! ... They hoped that I was DRACULA."

They met at Universal City in early 1932, while Karloff was shoot-ing *Night World*; in the surviving PR shots, the presence of these two powerhouses, clad in tuxedoes, is remarkable. A story in *Weird Tales* mag-azine (October 1932) claimed they had wagered as to who could scare the other to death, with Karloff climactically exclaiming: "You know me, Bela, you know me...And you shouldn't have made that foolish wager. Admit it, Bela!"

They then (according to *Weird Tales*) turned briefly into "two slimy, scaly monsters, dragon-like serpents, with blood-red, venomous eyes." Penny-dreadful stuff, of course, coupled with two stars fresh to Holly-wood celebrity, happy to oblige the PR squad. But the approach was profound: already, in the immediate wake of *Dracula* and *Frankenstein*, the audience realized the legendary stature of these men, their Poe-esque style...a sense of *immortality*.

Of course, every genre had its extremity; for horror in the early 1930s, it was Lionel Atwill, known as "Pinky" to his intimates—of which there were presumably many. The kinky "Pinky," in true life an aristo-cratic voluptuary, proclaiming his dramatic heroes to be Shakespeare's Hamlet ("with his pitiful diseased mind") and Richard III ("with his lust for killing and more killing"), won his horror superstardom in Warner Bros.' *Doctor X* and *Mystery of the Wax Museum*, and Majestic's *The Vam-pire Bat*. But he is perhaps at his most perversely vile in Paramount's *Murders in the Zoo*. In an episode still fascinating today, Atwill (who has just killed his wife's lover with mamba snake poison) moves in on his allegedly nymphomaniacal spouse—slinky Kathleen Burke ("Panther Woman" of Paramount's *Island of Lost Souls*). Atwill sensually cups his hand, and tantalizes the audience as he seems sure to be about to grasp Miss Burke's left breast. Then, in a sudden twist that must have amused the star (and relieved the actress), Atwill brings his hand to rest on her shoulder. It was just one of the tricks in Atwill's bizarre repertoire.

Of course, the ladies were a bit strange, too. Queen of 1930s horror was Fay Wray, *King Kong's* Delilah—wearing her blonde wig, giving that wide-eyed, open-mouthed, come-hither look, and unleashing that wild, orgasmic scream at the least provocation. In *Doctor X*, Wray is in her own Henna-rinsed hair, but that scream is there; in fact, she makes her entrance with that passionate wail—and for no real reason! Perhaps Wray's most perverse moment comes in *Mystery of the Wax Museum*; she cracks Atwill's wax mask—then, like a playgirl who has just discovered her lover is wearing a toupee, almost toyingly claws away at the broken mask. There stands Atwill, looking like a perfectly humiliated fried persimmon in his Westmore-applied makeup, as Wray gives one of her wildest theatre-rattling screams, gasping, "You fiend!" all the while clutching her breasts.

(Fay Wray—a legendary survivor of the era—probably didn't consciously bring these touches to her performances. In her 1989 memoir, *On the Other Hand*, she seems like a gallant, non-neurotic woman, who admits she was never even intrigued enough by the redoubtable Mr. Atwill to have a conversation with him. Yet, via the directors, writers, and style of 1930s horror, such was the end product of this Scream Queen's portrayals.)

In the early 1930s, Fay Wray had plenty of striking distaff company. There was the aforementioned Kathleen Burke, as the Panther Woman created by Charles Laughton's smarmy Dr. Moreau in *Island of Lost Souls*. Looking like a 1932 hooker dressed up for a "John" with a South Seas fetish, set up to mate with Richard Arlen, she capers through what Danny Peary (in his book *Guide for the Film Fanatic*) calls "one of the most repellent story lines in film history." Then there's Zita Johann, the sexy "Anckes-en-Amon" of *The Mummy*, festooned in long Egyptian wig and headdress and filmy gown, looking like she just sashayed off the stage of Cairo's Pink Pussycat strip joint—and acting with a sense of spirituality that must be seen to be believed. Karloff so soulfully plays his ardor for her that we never imagine just how humiliating it might have been had that poor, old, dried-and-crackly Mummy ever really tried to "have his way" with that nubile and ravishing reincarnation.

Of course, the impact made by the directors was legendary; unusual, brilliant men who gave these films sparks of their own offbeat personalities.

Frankenstein, an askew morality tale of souls and blasphemy, is the gospel according to Jimmy Whale—former actor/cartoonist/POW/stage manager/tango dancer, a gay genius with his own aura of alienation and loneliness. The mad little touches with which he cartooned *Frankenstein*, *The Old Dark House*, *The Invisible Man* and *Bride of Frankenstein* were very much a part of Whale himself, who would dress in his favorite suit to drown himself in his Pacific Palisades pool in 1957, and would leave behind a book on the bedstand: *Don't Drink the Water*.

And Tod Browning—"Bosco the Snake-Eater" and the "Hypnotic Living Corpse" of turn-of-the-century sideshows, who as part of his act would be buried alive for 48 hours; who directed such Lon Chaney silents as *The Unholy Three* and *London After Midnight*; who (for good or evil) directed Lugosi's *Dracula*. He was a man whose nostalgia for the sinister shadows of the carnival would climax with MGM's *Freaks* of 1932— an oeuvre overdose from which Browning never professionally recovered.

"In *Freaks* the movies make their great step toward national censorship," reported the Kansas City *Star*. "If they get it, they will have no one to blame but themselves."

The warning of censorship was not new; in fact, Kansas City had attacked *Frankenstein*, making *32* cuts—thereby slicing the running time in half and making the film nonsensical. (In the ensuing furor, the governor himself had to intervene, and *Frankenstein* was restored to its original version.) The gauntlet of national censorship had been thrown down as a threat—but, through the early 1930s, the dazzling variety of horrors just kept parading: MGM's *The Mask of Fu Manchu*, starring Karloff's gay dragon of a Fu, Myrna Loy as his sex-crazed daughter, and a bevy of dazzling Metro torture devices; Whale's *The Invisible Man* for Universal, with Claude Rains thrillingly planning his reign of terror, his "Invisible One" lamenting how uncomfortable it is when one has to terrorize while naked.

The 1930s Hollywood horror hit a crazy apex with *The Black Cat* (Universal, 1934): Karloff as a high priest of Lucifer, complete with a satanic hair-do and a hobby of keeping dead preserved blondes in vertical crystal caskets; Bela Lugosi as a mad psychiatrist who fears cats. Supposedly based on Poe's tale, the Edgar G. Ulmer directed/co-written/costumed/set designed masterwork featured none of Poe's plot, but plenty of his spirit: insanity, necrophilia, devil worship, and revenge. And, for the climax, there's a black mass, followed by Lugosi skinning alive a stripped-to-the-waist Karloff on his "own embalming rack"—the leading lady (Jacqueline Wells) watching and screaming like a perverse Pandora.

Karloff, Lugosi, and the recovered Wells all appeared at the May 3, 1934, Hollywood premiere of *The Black Cat*. Poe would be pleased; *The Black Cat* is Universal's hit of the season.

Enter the Hollywood Production Code.

One wonders if Cardinal Dougherty of Philadelphia had seen *The Black Cat* when, on June 8, 1934, he announced in his diocese a boycott of all movies, calling them "perhaps the greatest menace to faith and morals today." Nine days later, at a Cleveland rally, 50,000 Catholics took the pledge of the Legion of Decency to protest "indecent" films. And on July 6, 1934, Joseph Breen began his reign as lord and master of "the Hays Office," i.e., the Production Code Administration. It is a new world now, with a long list of no-nos; those flurries of stockings and lingerie Jacqueline Wells flashed in *The Black Cat* as she escaped the explosive climax with David Manners would never get by now.

The Hays Office was a power-to-be-feared. But if anyone expected horror's top movers and shakers to be intimidated—guess again.

January 2, 1935, and Universal begins *Bride of Frankenstein*—so audacious a fantasy that it presents Karloff as a Christ symbol, crucified on a pole in the forest. It is the mad masterpiece of James Whale, who also brings back "God" Colin Clive—more gaunt and twitchy than ever, a blasphemer as hooked on creating monsters as tragic Clive is on drinking himself to death. To play up the religious touch, Ernest Thesiger, as evil Dr. Pretorius, with pointed eyebrows and inflections, looks like the Devil; Valerie Hobson, as Elizabeth, in flowing hair and gowns, looks like an archangel. It is a crazy, sex/religion/romance opera, climaxed by Elsa Lanchester's bride—striking poses like an insane glamour girl, screaming in the face of her Monster bridegroom, mocking the Monster, Hollywood romance and creation itself all at once. Whale stocks the film with his old favorites like Una O'Connor (screaming maid Minnie) and Dwight Frye (prissy graverobber Karl) to make the lunacy complete; it is his final word on horror.

Bride of Frankenstein merrily escapes the Production Code censors— much to the Code's eventual embarrassment. Pennsylvania demands the cutting of the tag of Thesiger's line, "I also have created life as we say— *in God's own image*"; Ohio makes cuts; and in England, a censor decided that the scene of Karloff, gazing tenderly at the body of his bride-to-be, smacked of necrophilia. China agreed, and the International Censors cut the scene. Palestine and Hungary refused to show *Bride* at all.

The storm clouds gather, even as 1935 proves a classic year for horror. Universal's new Karloff and Bela Lugosi chiller, *The Raven*, comes-a-tapping; Canada cuts it to ribbons, the British censors remove 5 of its 61 minutes and Holland rejects it "because of degrading effect on the public." MGM's *Mad Love* offers a bald Peter Lorre giving mutilated pianist Colin Clive the hands of a guillotined murderer while lusting after his wife (Frances Drake, horror's most beautiful heroine); even the public rejects this one, and *Mad Love* loses $39,000.

"*Mad Love,*" wails the manager of Long Island's Suffolk Theatre in a lament to *Motion Picture Herald*, "is the type of picture that brought about censorship."

Time is running out. Universal still manages to squeeze out *Dracula's Daughter*, with Gloria Holden so lesbian-esque in the title role (especially in her infamous attack of Nan Gray) that her portrayal (seemingly overt today) probably went right over the head of many 1936 filmgoers *and* censors. Maybe the Production Code felt it necessary to cut *Dracula's Daughter* a break: it had impelled Universal to eliminate Dracula himself from the script (forcing a $4,000 payoff to Lugosi for *not* acting in the film) and a complete re-write. *Dracula's Daughter* signaled lights out for the genre's hallowed 1931 to 1936 era, and with it comes this question: How did these horror films ever pass censor muster at all?

Actually, there's a good answer: the most profound aspect of these horrors was that for all their challenges and defiance and quirky kinks they were remarkably *moral* films. They were often religious parables, with a firm belief and respect for the Divine, and as judgmental and dogmatic (at least in the final reel) as a first communion catechism. The shooting script of *Bride of Frankenstein* had offered an episode in which the Monster, coming across a grave marker of Christ on the cross, tried to save the figure from His crucifixion. If shot, and included in the release print, it might have crystallized the hallowed respect the genre held for Divinity.

Nevertheless, the curtain did indeed fall—and with a bang.

As detailed in this book, the 1937 British "H" certificate changed the course of Hollywood product, the style of horror, and the address of Bela Lugosi (who soon lost his Hollywood Hills mansion as work shriveled). The erratic Laemmles already had lost Universal City; for a strange time, it seemed that there was cosmic rejoicing over horror's doom, and the end of the whole sensational tone of 1930s movies. As if to symbolize it, Jean Harlow—Hollywood's most sexy star—died on a June morning in 1937 at the age of 26.

And, 18 June mornings later, Colin Clive, perhaps the most baroque of Hollywood's 1930s horror personalities, died—a victim of alcohol, tuberculosis and his own demons. Perhaps it was a blessing. What future could Clive (later hailed by Consumer Guide's *Rating the Movie Stars* as "the cinema's greatest sado-masochist") have in the new, homogenized we-love-Deanna Durbin movie capital?

A slow, almost underground comeback soon begins. In 1938, RKO re-releases *King Kong*, pruned by censors (scenes of Kong gobbling natives, stripping off Fay Wray's clothes and smelling his fingers, etc.); the double bill of *Dracula* and *Frankenstein* becomes a sensation.

And the resurrection comes: *Son of Frankenstein* (1939), Universal's Easter Sunday for horror, and a spectacular third entry in the Monster series. This box office smash forms a bridge from the 1930s horror to the 1940s, but its roots are definitely in the glory days. The barnstorming theatrics of Basil Rathbone as Wolf von Frankenstein, the magnificence of Lugosi's bearded, broken-necked "Old Ygor," the macabre humor of Lionel Atwill's one-armed Inspector Krogh—all are far more of the 1930s style of rich emoting than the subtle 1940s. And Karloff—screaming piteously to the heavens over the dead Ygor—gives the Frankenstein Monster his one last, great, heartbreaking moment in the movies. The audacity of Whale's misanthropic style is missing in the story, but lurking in the shadows: in the nooks and crannies of Jack Otterson's "Psychological sets," the epic sweep of director Rowland V. Lee's style and Frank Skinner's score and—perhaps most movingly—in the oil portrait of Colin Clive, above the blazing fireplace in the Frankenstein study.

Yet it is a new world of "Gods and Monsters," different from the one Ernest Thesiger's Pretorius had toasted in *Bride of Frankenstein*. Early 1930s audiences worshipped Garbo; early 1940s audiences would hail Betty Grable. This touch of the prosaic (along with the Breen Office's censorship vigilance) wreaks havoc with horror. Universal's *Black Friday* (1940), the studio's last Karloff and Lugosi movie, does something that would have been unthinkable in the 1930s: it does not put Boris and Bela together in a single scene. This gets by in 1940; it is a touch of discretion, keeping those two dynamos separated.

And these prosaics explain, partially anyway, the rise of Lon Chaney, Jr., as Universal's "master character creator" of the World War II years. Beefy young Lon, son of the late-lamented "Man of a Thousand Faces," is the horror star-next-door; he seems like a guy who can come home from playing the Wolf Man or Frankenstein's Monster or the Mummy or Dracula, grab a quick shower and take off for a night with the bowling league. He scores as *The Wolf Man* (1941), but totally lacks the Never-Never Land eccentricities of a Karloff or Lugosi. Atwill has more mystique in his toupee than Chaney has in his whole screen persona.

In a situation typical of forties horror, Stanley Ridges (front, as Prof. Kingsley) was the "monster" of *Black Friday* (1940), which happened to also feature Boris Karloff and Bela Lugosi.

Yet Lon's stolidity, his mundane talent, the very things that make him credible with the forties filmgoer. Ironically, Chaney—promoted by his studio as a ranchin', horse-lovin', regular kind-a-guy—is a violent, "sexually confused" alcoholic whose wife reportedly learned Judo to defend herself, and whose own son calls him "a drunken son of a bitch"; his life was a horror movie no 1940s producer would have touched.

As 1940s horror formulates, cracking and fissuring, the "King" is away: Karloff is the star of Broadway's super-hit *Arsenic and Old Lace*, which makes him a New York stage star, a good sport ("He said I looked like Boris Karloff!" says Boris, explaining why he killed a man) and rich (he owns a piece of the play) all at once.

In Karloff's absence, 1940s horror will still have its charms—such as Evelyn Ankers, Universal's "Queen of the Horrors," the beautiful blonde

Lon Chaney, Jr. as "Dynamo" Dan McCormick in *Man Made Monster* (1941). Chaney replaced the dark nuances of Karloff and Lugosi with his "average guy" persona and became the forties' biggest horror star.

Censors and watchdogs barely noticed the Frankenstein Monster (Lon Chaney, Jr.) in his fourth outing, *The Ghost of Frankenstein* (shown here with Cedric Hardwicke as the creator's second son).

The Great Solvani (Cecil Kellaway), Dr. Petrie (Charles Trowbridge), and Steve Banning (Dick Foran) inspect Kharis (Tom Tyler) in *The Mummy's Hand* **(1940), a typically entertaining but nonconfrontational forties horror.**

who unleashes her magnificent scream in so many melodramas. One wishes to see her strut her stuff opposite Karloff or Lugosi, but it is Chaney who lumbers on, Universal's all-purpose ghoul of the forties. He is worthy as *The Wolf Man*, finding his own stardust and folklore under Universal's full moon. But as the Monster in *The Ghost of Frankenstein*, he is none too exciting. Hans J. Salter, whose thrilling music does so much for Universal horror of the forties, gives Chaney's Monster a *Doooo*-be-do, *Doooo*-be-do, *Doooo*-be-do leitmotif which (appropriately) sounds like Saturday morning cartoon music for a fat smurf.

Universal considers Lugosi too strange (and probably too old) for leads; he only gets supporting roles at the studio, although when he gets a good one—e.g., Ygor in *The Ghost of Frankenstein*—he emerges as the star. Lugosi must drop by Monogram to get leads, working for producer "Jungle Sam" Katzman, King of the Hollywood Yahoos, peddling movies

Lon Chaney, Jr. as the Count in *Son of Dracula* (1943), one of the forties' few kinky horrors.

Irena (**Simone Simon**) and Amy (**Ann Carter**) straddle the corpse of Julia Farren (**Julia Dean**) in Val Lewton's *The Curse of the Cat People* (1944). This misleadingly titled picture was actually a thought provoking study of a child's fantasy life.

like *The Ape Man* (1943), the climax of which finds lovely Louise Currie lashing poor, hairy Bela with a whip.

And, speaking of whips, Lionel Atwill leers as only he can in *Man Made Monster* (1941), then life imitates art: he hosts that infamous Yuletide orgy in his Pacific Palisades house, and becomes star of a real-life Hollywood scandal. Atwill occasionally gives flashes of his old, flamboyantly vile self—a mad doctor in *The Ghost of Frankenstein*, Moriarty in *Sherlock Holmes and the Secret Weapon*—but he has to tone down his act; the headlines are juicy enough.

Once in a while comes a sophisticated, deluxe horror movie such as MGM's *Dr. Jekyll and Mr. Hyde* (1941): Spencer Tracy's sexually sadistic Hyde, a Freudian dream montage (Ingrid Bergman being shoved by a

The Frankenstein Monster (Bela Lugosi) was scaring no one by this time, as he "menaces" Ilona Massey in *Frankenstein Meets the Wolf Man* (1943).

giant corkscrew into a bottle which, of course, explodes, etc.), an accent on souls and a finale of celestial forgiveness all make this a winner (despite Tracy's personal horror at his own performance). But horror movies of the 1940s are a commodity. As Jungle Sam Katzman prospers, James Whale has retired to the Palisades, Tod Browning to Malibu. Victor Fleming (Oscar winner for *Gone With the Wind*) directs MGM's *Dr. Jekyll and Mr. Hyde*, but do not expect him to make another horror film. The domain belongs now to slick pros like Erle C. Kenton, who will bring in a picture right on schedule and budget.

Actually, there are some richly creative, suggestive and frightening horror movies being made—namely, by young producer Val Lewton at RKO. His premiere production, *Cat People* (1942), is a show biz sleeper, with an incredible premise: a bride cannot have sex with her husband. Is it because she is a cat woman? Or is she frigid? Or is she a lesbian? (Or is she a frigid lesbian?) Lewton, star Simone Simon and the company keep everybody guessing as this horror movie—giving the crowds the kind of chills and spice they truly want and earning $4 million internationally. Lewton escapes RKO front office dictates and the Production Code by a simple trick: his films have *no monsters*. Hence Lewton can get away with a film like *The Seventh Victim* (1943), in which Jean Brooks plays a devil worshipper who wears a Cleopatra wig and hangs herself.

It seems that indignities fall upon the heads of many of the 1930s Great Ones: *Frankenstein Meets the Wolf Man* (1943), e.g., casts Lugosi in the Monster role he'd scorned in 1931. He humbly takes the part at the 11th hour, only after Universal decides it is too troublesome to have Chaney play both Monster *and* Wolf Man, as originally planned. Bela collapses on the set under the makeup and costume. He sees much of his role played by a stunt man. And after it is all over, Universal cuts his Monster dialogue, and references to the Monster's blindness, making Bela's Monster a bolt-necked farce. And there's another death: Dwight Frye, giggling Renfield of *Dracula*, hunchback Fritz of *Frankenstein*, supporting player in so many other horror shows (including *Frankenstein Meets the Wolf Man*). At the time Frye dies in 1943, of a heart attack at age 44, he is earning his primary income as a tool designer at Douglas Aircraft.

Mediocrity rules. Universal's *Son of Dracula* (1943) has a honey of a vampire *femme fatale* (Louise Allbritton) and fine direction by Robert Siodmak; but our Dracula (or, as he spells it backwards, Alucard) is Lon Chaney, plump and piggy-eyed. In the original *Dracula*, Bela had those three brides slinking in the castle; in *Son of Dracula*, Lon has only one—

Bela Lugosi as Armand Tesla, Dracula clone, with Nina Foch in *The Return of the Vampire* (1944), the Count himself would appear four times during the forties, lastly and pointedly in *Abbott and Costello Meet Frankenstein* (1948).

and he must take her to a justice of the peace to make it legal. Censorship has made its mark.

Then, out of the blue, comes 20th Century–Fox's *The Lodger* (1944). While the censors wail that Merle Oberon and her Can-Can girls cannot show the tops of their stockings or garters while performing "the Parisian Trot," Laird Cregar, Fox's young, 260-pound character star, plays Jack the Ripper as a homosexual poseur, even inferring an incestuous love for his dead brother. Cregar's sly performance shocks his bisexual friend Tyrone Power (then in the Marines) with its out-of-the-closet boldness; his theatrics are dazzling, and as Cregar makes a personal appearance at *The Lodger*'s opening at New York's Roxy Theatre, the audience awards him a five-minute ovation.

Boris Karloff as *The Body Snatcher* **(1945), one of the few forties horror movies to equal the artistry and dark thrills of the thirties classics.**

But, a sign of the times: Laird Cregar is not happy in the 1940s as a gay actor *or* a screen villain. While playing a madman in Fox's *Hangover Square*, he diets so mercilessly, hoping to change his sexual and dramatic type, that he dies at age 31. *Hangover Square* premieres after his death.

Chaney keeps shuffling in Universal's Mummy series, telling a reporter on the set that Mummy movies are for "nuts." Jungle Sam Katzman produces Monogram's *Voodoo Man*, proudly describing the film in an interview as "a moron picture." *Voodoo Man* takes it easy on Bela (quite dashing as a goateed sorcerer), but merrily debases two of the 1940s' best actors: John Carradine (cast here as "Toby," lecherous, bongo-playing chief moron of this moron picture) and George Zucco (as the chanting, war-painted-and-feathered high priest of Ramboona). The actors at least have the right idea: Zucco takes his pay and buys more animals for his ranch; Carradine grabs his *Voodoo Man* check, runs off to San Francisco and stars in his own Shakespearean company as Hamlet.

Inevitably, it comes to the "Monster Rally"—Universal's *House of Frankenstein* (1944). The movie is actually a circus, with ringmaster Karloff (back from *Arsenic and Old Lace*, and complete with top hat) and—in the 3-rings—John Carradine's Dracula, Lon Chaney's Wolf Man and Glenn Strange's Frankenstein Monster. (A bonus attraction: J. Carrol Naish as a hunchback.) Eight of the principals die in the film (a dead heat with Shakespeare's bloodbath, *Hamlet*); the censors let it slide, as long as most of the actual deaths occur in shadow or off-screen. Indeed, the Breen Office seems more concerned with Elena Verdugo keeping any "suggestive moves" out of her Gypsy dance.

Then, again, a thunderbolt: *The Body Snatcher* (RKO, 1945). From the virtual ashes of Hollywood horror rises the greatest terror movie of the 1940s: Karloff (magnificent in his title role) and Lugosi (effective in his creepy cameo), a Gothic story (by Robert Louis Stevenson), and the atmospherics and poetics of producer Val Lewton. Robert Wise, fated to win four Oscars, directs. And, in the grand tradition of 1930s horror classics, the film has censorship trouble. Ohio condemns it in its entirety until cuts are made; the Catholic Legion of Decency labels it "Objectionable in Part, due to excessive gruesomeness"; and Great Britain actually cuts Karloff's climactic apparition—robbing the film of climax *and* moral!

Yet a classic had come to pass, making it easier to accept Universal's new "monster rally," *House of Dracula*. It rewards "master character creator" Lon Chaney with a cure for his werewolvery, but ruthlessly kills off Dracula (Carradine), the Monster (Strange), the Mad Doctor (Onslow

Stevens) and even the sweet, little hunchbacked nurse (Jane Adams). Curiously it also kills off Lionel Atwill, as a police inspector. Significantly, in the wake of Atwill's "orgy trial" (he had been convicted of perjury, then managed to have it overturned on a technicality), Universal had cast him as an inspector in both *House of Frankenstein* and *House of Dracula*—"safe" roles which gave no room for leers. Yet in *House of Dracula*, for no dramatic reason, Atwill's character is killed off anyway.

Apparently, at this point, Universal was taking no chances.

A few more horror films eked their way into theatres in the wake of World War II; many consider the best of this "last gasp" bunch to have been *Bedlam* (1946)—a great villainous role for Karloff, a crusading leading lady in Anna Lee, and a humanitarian theme movingly played up by Val Lewton. And there's another death, to mark the times: on April 22, 1946, three days after the New York premiere of *Bedlam*, Lionel Atwill dies of cancer.

Others consider the curtain to have dropped definitively with Universal-International's *Abbott and Costello Meet Frankenstein* (1948)—the comics cavorting with Chaney's Wolf Man, Strange's Monster and Lugosi's Dracula.

At any rate, the horrors of the 1930s and 1940s soon were in vaults, buried alive, waiting for "a new life to come," as Colin Clive had said in *Frankenstein*. It would be a "new life" of Realart re-releases, TV's *Shock! Theatre*, and, finally, the Video Age. Who could have predicted so glorious an afterlife of these horror films and their creators?

Surely not the censors.

Epilogue

The horror genre, after losing most of its bite and brilliance during the forties, ground to a second halt after World War II ended. The *real* horror of the war, plus the threat posed by the new atomic age, made Dracula look a bit silly. As in 1936, audiences began to tire of the same old thing; *film noir*, which incorporated some horror elements, took up the slack. The merger of Universal with International Pictures in July 1946, did not help matters either, since the resulting company (Universal-International) wanted to produce upscale movies instead of programmers.

Despite all this, the BBFC *still* had its hands full of horrors at the decade's end, since restrictions caused by the war held up the UK release of pictures made in the early forties. Oddly, the British were still dealing with censorship problems posed by horrifics several years after Hollywood quit making them.

By 1950, the "H" certificate was considered to be no longer viable and, on January 1, 1951, was replaced by the "X." The BBFC described this new category as "incorporating the old 'H' certificate, and specifically limiting audiences to those of 16 years or older. The new category was not for merely sordid films dealing with unpleasant subjects, but films which, while not being suitable for children, are good adult entertainment and films which appeal to an intelligent public."

The new "X" began to get a workout when the third wave of horror movies began, more or less kick-started by Britain's own Hammer Films. Censors, critics, and audiences alike were shocked into insensibility by *The Curse of Frankenstein* (1957), which added a few new twists—color photography, plenty of blood and severed limbs, low-cut gowns—to the

The Baron (Peter Cushing) and Paul (Robert Urquhart), his rebellious collaborator, hunt for the Creature in *The Curse of Frankenstein* (1957). It was open season on the movie, too.

old mix. Peter Cushing's cold-hearted baron and Christopher Lee's road-accident monster proved to be too much for British critics, notably C.A. Lejune: "I should rank [it] among the half dozen most repulsive films I have encountered" (*The Observer*, May 5). Many whined for the good old days of "wholesome" shockers like the original *Frankenstein*, forgetting (or, more likely, unaware of) the firestorm *that* film had created. Still, *The Curse of Frankenstein* was, and is, fairly rough—as were other Hammers (*Horror of Dracula*, 1958, *The Curse of the Werewolf*, 1961) that followed. In the United States, with no rating system, any child old enough to find his or her way to the theatre could legally receive some nasty shocks; British children were protected by the "X."

As the BBFC pointed out, the "X" did not just cover horrifics, but also intelligent adult drama like *Room at the Top* (1959) featuring Laurence Harvey as Joe Lampton, an amoral monster more horrifying than Dracula.

Critics and censors were horrified by the Baron (Peter Cushing) and his Creature (Christopher Lee) in *The Curse of Frankenstein* (1957) which matched the reaction to the supposedly tame *Frankenstein* a quarter of a century earlier.

"This is in no sense a 'U' story," said the *Sunday Express* (January 1959), "but it is real and straightforward and rings true. In this case at least, and at last, the "X" certificate looks like a badge of honour."

This aside, there were plenty of horror movies to confound the BBFC in addition to Hammer's assault; the American-International Vincent Price/Edgar Allan Poe series and the Amicus multi-part horrors, were among the most noticeable. Due to the new freedom and frankness available to filmmakers, the horror movies became more and more violent, and sex became more common as a plot device. This was also true of mainstream pictures.

To combat these excesses, the BBFC revamped its categories in July 1970:

U—As before.

A—Becomes advisory. It permits children of five years of age, whether accompanied or not, but warns parents that a film in this category may contain some material that some parents might prefer for their children under 14 years of age not to see.

AA—Allows the admission of children of 14 years or over, whether accompanied or not.

X—As before, except that the age limit for admission is raised from 16 years to 18 years.

During the seventies, horror movies continued to get more horrible, led by the example set by *The Exorcist* (1973), which inspired other satanically oriented pictures of far less quality. Mainstream films (*Straw Dogs*, 1971) also continued the excessive violence, and the BBFC apparently found its labeling inadequate. A new, more complex rating system was instituted on November 1, 1982, in which the "X" was phased out:

U—As before.

PG—Parental guidance. General viewing, but some scenes may be unsuitable for young children.

15—Suitable for persons of 15 years and over.

18—Suitable for persons of 18 years and over.

R18—Restricted. Approved in principal. For restricted distribution only, through specially licensed premises to which no one under 18 is admitted.

With children constantly being exposed to more explicit material in films, the system became even *more* complex on August 1, 1989, when the "12" category was introduced: "Passed only for persons of twelve years and over. No person apparently under the age of 12 years shall be admitted to any exhibition."

But, no matter how encompassing its ratings became, the BBFC found it difficult to keep up with the audiences' desire for horrific pictures. The video revolution of the mid-eighties made it possible for a child to see practically *anything* on home television. To counter this new censorial snafu, the BBFC instituted the Video Records Act of 1984: "It was a principal purpose of the Act to regulate the distribution of video recordings by extending to video the long familiar system of classification which applies in the cinema."

Added to the cinema classification was the "Uc," which "distinguished recordings intended particularly for young children from those which are marketed for the whole family."

The BBFC's general position was: "The fundamental principal of film and video classification is still the protection of children." A new danger for young viewers was the "video nasty." The board's position on this aberration was *quite* clear: "The term 'video nasties' was introduced to Britain in the spring of 1982, when it was coined by the press to describe the sudden fashion for this new form of violent entertainment, much of it offensively advertised, most of it never certified for cinema, and all of it apparently available in unregulated form to children of any age. The arrival in so many British homes of a great many unclassified video cassettes brought home to many responsible adults the unrealized dangers of some forms of violent and sadistic entertainment on which no limits whatever had been set."

The board then united obscenity with violence: "A work is likely to be regarded as obscene if it portrays violence to such a degree and so explicitly that its appeal can only be to those who are disposed to derive positive enjoyment from seeing such violence."

Is there a direct correlation between *Bride of Frankenstein* and "video nasties"? Are children harmed by the horrific? How much is too much? The BBFC today feels that, "Some forms of terror or horror will continue to give audiences much the same sort of thrill as the screams of delight on a fun fair ride. Children have always liked ghost stories, and even adults like the surge of adrenaline that comes from braving the worst that film-makers can throw at them, always provided there is a sufficiently safe and distancing element of make-believe. But the key factor here is that the audience's sympathies and identification are not with the aggressor, but with the innocent hero or heroine who is trying, against all odds, to escape the forces of evil, whether real or supernatural."

Two things seem to be clear in this intricate history of British censorship vs. horror: (1) In most cases, the censors were (and are) sincere in their desire to protect children, and (2) No matter what restrictions are placed upon them, horror movies were (and will be) attractive to young audiences.

In its review of Hammer's *The Man Who Could Cheat Death*, *Variety* (June 24, 1959) noted "invention and embellishment in this field appear to have been exhausted. As even greater horror is required, there is less and less that is horrible enough." Oddly, this perceptive view could just as easily have been applied to *Dracula's Daughter* or to *Silence of the Lambs* (1991). When, if ever, will that point be reached?

Despite the many attempts to restrict or even ban horror movies, no *conclusive* evidence exists to prove that they are responsible for aberrant behavior or emotional problems in children or adults. The so-called "horror ban of 1937" did little to end their production; horror movies survived the Depression, World War II, and everything since. They will likely survive as long as there are movies and people to watch them. And, it is just as likely that censors, watch-dogs, and critics will continue to call for their demise.

Filmography

DRACULA (1931 USA)

Released February 14, 1931; A Universal Picture; *Director*: Tod Browning; *Producer*: Carl Laemmle, Jr.; *Associate Producer*: E.M. Asher; *Screenplay*: Garrett Fort, based on Bram Stoker's novel and Hamilton Dean's and John L. Balderson's play; *Director of Photography*: Karl Freund: *Art Director*: Charles B. Hall; *Editor*: Milton Carruth; *Supervising Editor*: Maurice Pivar; *Set Designers*: Herman Rosse and John Hoffman; *Effects*: Frank J. Booth; *Music Conductor*: Heinz Roemheld; *Set Decorator*: Russell A. Gausman; *Costumes*: Ed Ware, Vera West; *Makeup*: Jack P. Pierce; *Sound Recording*: C. Roy Runter; *Continuity*: Dudley Murphy; 75 minutes; BBFC Certificate: A.

Bela Lugosi (Dracula), Helen Chandler (Mina), David Manners (Harker), Dwight Frye (Renfield), Edward Van Sloan (Van Helsing), Herbert Bunston (Dr. Seward, Frances Dade (Lucy), Joan Standing (The Maid), Charles Gerrard (Martin), Moon Carroll (Briggs), Josephine Velez (Grace), Michael Visaroff (Innkeeper), Daisy Belmore, Nicholas Bela, Donald Murphy (Coach Passengers), Carla Laemmle (Girl), Tod Browning (Harbor Master).

FRANKENSTEIN (1931 USA)

Released November 21, 1931; A Universal Picture; *Director*: James Whale; *Producer*: Carl Laemmle, Jr.; *Screenplay*: Garrett Fort, Francis Edwards, based on John L. Balderston's composition; Adapted from Mary W. Shelley's novel and Peggy Webling's play; *Director of Photography*: Arthur Edeson; *Associate Producer*: E.M. Asher; *Editor*: Clarence Kolster; *Supervising Editor*: Maurice Pivar; *Art Director*: Charles D. Hall; *Sound*: C. Roy Hunter; *Set Design*: Herman Rosse; *Makeup*: Jack P. Pierce; *Special Electrical Effects*: Kenneth Strickfaden, Frank Graves, Raymond Lindsay; *Continuity*: Thomas Reed; *Technical Advisor*: Dr. Cecil Reynolds; *Music*: David Broekman;

Props: Eddie Keys; *Script Editor*: Richard L. Schayer; 71 minutes; BBFC Certificate: A.

Colin Clive (Henry Frankenstein), Mae Clark (Elizabeth), John Boles (Victor Moritz), Boris Karloff (The Monster), Edward Van Sloan (Dr. Waldman), Frederick Kerr (Baron Frankenstein), Dwight Frye (Fritz), Lionel Belmore (The Burgomaster), Marilyn Harris (Little Maria), Michael Mark (Ludwig), Arletta Duncan, Pauline Moore (Bridesmaids), Francis Ford (Hans).

DR. JEKYLL AND MR. HYDE (1931 USA)

Released December 31, 1931; A Paramount Release; *Director*: Rouben Mamoulian; *Producer*: Rouben Mamoulian; *Screenplay:* Samuel Hoffenstein and Percy Heath, based on Robert Louis Stevenson's story; *Director of Photography*: Karl Struss; *Art Director*: Hans Drier; *Editor*: William Shea; *Makeup*: Wally Westmore; *Costumes*: Travis Banton; 98 minutes; BBFC Certificate: A.

Frederic March (Jekyll/Hyde), Miriam Hopkins (Ivy), Rose Hobart (Muriel), Holmes Herbert (Dr. Lanyon), Halliwell Hobbes (Carew), Edgar Norton (Poole), Tempe Pigott (Mrs. Hawkins), Eric Wilton (Briggs), Arnold Lucy (Utterson), Douglas Walton (Student), Murdock Mac Quarrie (Doctor), John Rogers (Waiter), Sam Harris (Dancer).

FREAKS (1932 USA)

Released February 20, 1932; A Metro-Goldwyn-Mayer Release; *Director*: Tod Browning; *Screenplay*: Willis Goldbeck and Leon Gordon, based on Clarence Robbins' story; *Dialogue*: Edgar Allan Wolf, Al Boasberg; *Director of Photography*: Merritt B. Gerstad; *Art Directors*: Cedric Gibbons, Merrill Pye; *Editor*: Basil Wrangell; *Sound*: Gavin Burns; *Production Manager*: Harry Sharrock; *Assistant Director*: Errol Taggert; 64 minutes; BBFC Certificate: Not granted.

Wallace Ford (Phroso), Leila Hyams (Venus), Olga Baclanova (Cleopatra), Rosco Ates (Roscoe), Henry Victor (Hercules), Harry Earles (Hans), Daisy Earles (Frieda), Rose Dione (Madame Tetrallini), Daisy and Violet Hilton (Siamese Twins), Schlitze (Herself), Josephine Joseph (Half Woman/Half Man), Johnny Eck (Half Boy), Frances O'Connor (Armless Girl), Peter Robinson (Human Skeleton), Olga Roderick (Bearded Lady), Koo Koo (Herself), Prince Randian (Living Torso), Martha Morris (Armless Girl), Zip and Pip (Pinheads), Elizabeth Green (Stork Woman), Angelo Rossitto (Angeleno), Edward Brophy, Mat McHugh (Rollo Brothers), Albert Conti (Monsieur Duval), Michael Visaroff (Jean), Ernie S. Adams (Sideshow Patron), Murray Kinell (Barker).

MURDERS IN THE RUE MORGUE (1932 USA)

Released February 21, 1932; A Universal Picture; *Director*: Robert Florey; *Producer*: Carl Laemmle, Jr.; *Associate Producer*: E.M. Asher;

Screenplay: Tom Reed and Dale van Every, based on Edgar Allan Poe's story; *Director of Photography*: Karl Freund; *Art Director*: Charles D. Hall; *Editor*: Milton Carruth; *Supervising Editor*: Maurice Pivar; *Musical Director*: Heinz Roemheld; *Special Effects*: John P. Fulton; *Special Process*: Frank Williams; *Story Adaptation*: Robert Florey; *Makeup*: Jack P. Pierce; *Set Designer*: Herman Rosse; *Assistant Directors*: Scott Beal, Joseph McDonough, Charles S. Gould; *Technical Advisor*: Howard Salemson; *Additional Dialogue*: John Huston; 62 minutes; BBFC Certificate: A.

Sidney Fox (Camille), Bela Lugosi (Dr. Mirakle), Leon Waycoff (Dupin), Bert Roach (Paul), Betsy Ross Clarke (Mme L'Espanaye), Brandon Hurst (Prefect of Police), D'Arcy Corrigan (Morgue Keeper), Noble Johnson (Janos), Arlene Francis (Woman of the Streets), Edna Marion (Mignette), Charlotte Henry, Polly Ann Young (Girls), Herman Bing (Franz Odenheimer), Agostino Borgato (Montani), Harry Holman (Landlord), Torben Meyer (The Dane), John T. Murray, Christian Frank (Gendarmes), D. Vernon (Tenant), Michael Visaroff, Ted Billings (Men), Charles T. Millsfield (Bearded Man), Monte Montague (Workman), Charles Gemora (Erik), Hamilton Green (Barker), Tempe Pigott (Crone).

WHITE ZOMBIE (1932 USA)

Released July 28, 1932; A United Artists Release of a Halperin Brothers Production; *Director*: Victor Halperin; *Producer*: Edward Halperin;

Screenplay: Garnett Weston; *Photography*: Arthur Martinelli; *Editor*: Howard McLernon; *Makeup*: Jack P. Pierce; *Music*: Guy B. Williams, Xavier Cugat, Nathaniel Dett, Gaston Borch; *Assistant Director*: William Cody; 69 minutes; BBFC Certificate: A.

Bela Lugosi (Murder), Madge Bellamy (Madeline), Joseph Cawthorne (Dr. Brunet), Robert Frazer (Beaumont), John Harron (Neil), Bandon Hurst (Silver), George Burr MacAnna (Von Gelder), Frederick Peters (Chauvin), Annette Stone (Maid), John Printz (Latour), Dan Crimmins (Pierre), Claude Morgan, John Fergusson (Zombies), Velma Gresham (Maid), Clarence Muse (Driver).

THE OLD DARK HOUSE (1932 USA)

Released October 20, 1932; A Universal Picture; *Director*: James Whale; *Producer*: Carl Laemmle, Jr.; *Screenplay*: Benn W. Levy, based on J.B. Priestley's **Benighted**; *Additional Dialogue*: R.C. Sherriff; *Director of Photography*: Arthur Edeson; *Editor*: Clarence Kolster; *Art Director*: Charles D. Hall; *Music*: Bernhard Kaun; *Sound*: William Hedgcock; *Makeup*: Jack P. Pierce; *Assistant Director*: Joseph A. McDonough; 71 minutes; BBFC Certificate: A.

Boris Karloff (Morgan), Melvyn Douglas (Roger Penderel), Charles Laughton (Sir William Porterhouse), Gloria Stuart (Margaret), Raymond Massey (Philip), Ernest Thesiger (Horace Femm), Lilian

Bond (Gladys), Eva Moore (Rebecca Femm), Brember Wills (Saul Femm), Elspeth Dudgeon (Sir Roderick Femm).

THE MASK OF FU MANCHU (1932 USA)

Released November 1932; An MGM Production; *Director*: Charles Brabin; *Producer*: Irving Thalberg; *Screenplay*: Irene Kuhn, Edgar Allan Woolf, John Willard, based on Sax Rohmer's novel; *Photography*: Tony Gaudio; *Editor*: Ben Lewis; *Art Director*: Cedric Gibbons; *Costumes*: Adrian; 72 minutes (65 min. UK); BBFC Certificate: A.

Boris Karloff (Fu Manchu), Lewis Stone (Nayland Smith), Karen Morley (Sheila Barton), Myrna Loy (Fah Lo See), Charles Starrett (Terry Granville), Jean Hersholt (Von Berg), Lawrence Grant (Sir Lionel Barton), David Torrence (McLeod).

THE MUMMY (1932 USA)

Released December 22, 1932; A Universal Picture; *Director*: Karl Freund; *Producer*: Carl Laemmle, Jr.; *Associate Producer*: Stanley Bergerman; *Screenplay*: John L. Balderston, based on a story by Nina Wilcox Putnam and Richard Schayer; *Director of Photography*: Charles Stumar; *Editor*: Milton Carruth; *Makeup*: Jack P. Pierce; *Art Director*: Willy Pogany; *Special Effects*: John P. Fulton; *Music*: James Dietrich; 72 minutes; BBFC Certificate: A.

Boris Karloff (Imhotep/Ardath Bey), Zita Johann (Helen Grosvenor/Anck-es-en-Amon), David

Manners (Frank Whemple), Edward Van Sloan (Dr. Muller), Arthur Byron (Sir Joseph Whemple), Bramwell Fletcher (Norton), Noble Johnson (The Nubian), Kathryn Byron (Frau Muller), Leonard Mudie (Professor Pearson), Eddie Kane (Dr. LeBarron), Tony Marlow (Inspector), Pat Somerset (Dancing Partner), C. Montague Shaw, Leland Hodgson (Small Talkers), Gordon Elliott (Dancer); these performers did not appear in the release print: James Crane (King Amerophis), Henry Victor (Saxon Warrior), Arnold Grey (Knight).

ISLAND OF LOST SOULS (1933 USA)

Released January 11, 1933; A Paramount Production; *Director*: Erle C. Kenton; *Screenplay*: Waldemar Young, Philip Wylie; *Novel*: H.G. Wells' *Island of Dr. Moreau*; *Director of Photography*: Karl Struss; *Art Director*: Hans Dreier; *Special Effects*: Gordon Jennings; *Makeup*: Wally Westmore; 72 minutes; BBFC Certificate: Not Granted.

Charles Laughton (Dr. Moreau), Richard Arlen (Edwin Parker), Leila Hyams (Ruth Thomas), Bela Lugosi (Sayer of the Law), Kathleen Burke (Lota), Arthur Hohl (Montgomery), Stanley Fields (Capt. Davies), Paul Hurst (Donohue), Hans Steinke (Ouran), Tetsu Komai (M'Ling), George Irving (Consul).

MYSTERY OF THE WAX MUSEUM (1933 USA)

Released February 16, 1933; A Warner Bros. Release; *Director*: Michael Curtiz; *Screenplay*: Don Mullaly, Carl Erickson; *Original Story*: Charles S. Belden; *Director of Photography*: Ray Rennahan; *Camera*: Dick Towers; *Art Director*: Anton Grot; *Editor*: George Amy; *Makeup*: Perc Westmore; *Gowns:* Orry-Kelly; *Wax Figures*: L.E. Otis, H. Clay Campell; Color; 79 minutes; BBFC Certificate: A.

Lionel Atwill (Ivan Igor), Fay Wray (Charlotte Duncan), Glenda Farrell (Florence), Frank McHugh (Jim), Allen Vincent (Ralph Burton), Gavin Gordon (George Winton), Edwin Maxwell (Joe Worth), Holmes Herbert (Dr. Rasmussen), Claude King (Golatily), Arthur Edmund Carew (Professor D'Arcy), Thomas Jackson (Detective), De-Witt Jennings (Police Captain), Matthew Betz (Hugo), Monica Bannister (Joan Gale).

KING KONG (1933 USA)

Released March 2, 1933; An RKO Production; *Directors*: Merian C. Cooper, Ernest B. Schoedsack; *Producers*: Cooper, Schoedsack; *Screenplay*: James Creelman, Ruth Rose (based on an idea by Cooper and Edgar Wallace); *Directors of Photography*: Eddie Linden, Vernon Walker, J. O.Taylor; *Chief Technician*: Willis O'Brien; *Art Technicians*: Mario Larrinaga, Byron L. Crabbe; *Technical Staff*: E. B. Gibson, Marcel Delgado, Fred Reese, Orville Goldner, Carroll Shepphird; *Sets*: Carroll Clark, Al Herman; *Editor*: Ted Cheesman; *Music*: Max Steiner; *Sound Effects*: Murray Spivack; *Production Assistants*: Archie F. Marshek, Walter Daniels; 100 minutes; BBFC Certificate: A.

Fay Wray (Ann Darrow), Robert Armstrong (Carl Denham), Bruce Cabot (John Driscoll), Frank Reicher (Capt. Englehorn), Sam Hardy (Charles Weston), Nobel Johnson (Native Chief), Steve Clemento (Witch King), James Flavin (Second Mate), and "King Kong."

MURDERS IN THE ZOO (1933 USA)

Released March 31, 1933; A Paramount Production; *Director*: Edward Sutherland; *Associate Producer*: E. Lloyd Sheldon; *Screenplay*: Philip Wylie, Seton J. Miller; *Additional Dialogue*: Milton H. Gropper; *Director of Photography*: Ernest Haller; 61 minutes; BBFC Certificate: A.

Charlie Ruggles (Peter Yates), Lionel Atwill (Eric Gorman), Gial Patrick (Jerry Evans), Randolph Scott (Dr. Woodford), John Lodge (Roger Hewitt), Kathleen Burke (Evelyn Gorman), Harry Beresford (Prof. Evans).

THE GHOUL (1933 UK)

Released July 24, 1933; A Gaumont British Production; *Director*: T. Hayes Hunter; *Producer*: Michael Balcon; *Screenplay*: Roland Pertwee, John Hastings Turner; Adapted by Rupert Downing from the novel by Frank King and Leonard Hines; *Director of Photography*: Gunther Krampf; *Music*: Louis Levy; *Art Director*: Alfred Junge; *Editors*: Ian Dalrymple, Ralph Kemplen; *Makeup*: Heinrich Heitfeldt; 80 minutes; BBFC Certificate: A.

Boris Karloff (Prof. Morlant), Cedric Hardwicke (Broughton),

Ernest Thesiger (Laing), Dorothy Hyson (Betty Harlon), Anthony Bushell (Ralph Morlant), Kathleen Harrison (Kaney), Harold Huth (Aga Ben Dragore), D.A. Clark-Smith (Mahmoud), Ralph Richardson (Nigel Hartley), Jack Raine (Chauffeur).

THE INVISIBLE MAN (1933 USA)

Released November 12, 1933; A Universal Picture; *Director*: James Whale; *Producer*: Carl Laemmle, Jr.; *Screenplay*: R.C. Sherriff, based on H.G. Wells' **The Invisible Man**; *Director of Photography*: Arthur Edeson; *Art Director*: Charles D. Hall; *Special Effects*: John P. Fulton; *Editor*: Ted Kent; *Makeup*: Jack P. Pierce; *Music*: W. Franke Harling; *Special Photography*: John Mescall; 70 minutes; BBFC Certificate: A.

Claude Rains (Griffin), Gloria Stuart (Flora), William Harrigan (Dr. Kemp), Henry Travers (Dr. Cranley), Una O'Connor (Mrs. Hall), Forrester Harvey (Mr. Hall), Holmes Herbert (Chief of Police), E.E. Clive (Constable Jaffers), Dudley Digges (Chief of Detectives), Harry Stubbs (Inspector Bird), Donald Stuart (Inspector Lane), Merle Tottenham (Milly), Walter Brennan (Man on Bicycle), Dwight Frye (Reporter), Jameson Thomas, Craufurd Kent (Doctors), John Peter Richmond [John Carradine] (Informer), John Merivale (Newsboy), Violet Kemble Cooper (Woman), Robert Brower (Farmer), Bob Reeves, Jack Richardson, Robert Adair (Officials), Monte Montague (Policeman), Ted Billings, D'Arcy Corrigan (Villagers).

THE BLACK CAT (1934 USA)

Released May 7, 1934; A Universal Picture; *Director*: Edgar G. Ulmer; *Producer*: Carl Laemmle, Jr.; *Supervising Producer*: E.M. Asher; *Screenplay*: Peter Ruric (suggested by Edgar Allan Poe's short story); *Director of Photography*: John J. Mescall; *Art Director*: Charles D. Hall; *Editor*: Ray Curtiss; *Assistant Directors*: W.J. Reiter, Sam Weisenthal; *Special Effects*: John P. Fulton; *Makeup*: Jack P. Pierce; *Camera*: King Gray; *Musical Director*: Heinz Roemheld; *Continuity*: Tom Kilpatrick; 65 minutes; UK title: **House of Doom**; BBFC Certificate: A.

Boris Karloff (Poelzig), Bela Lugosi (Werdegast), David Manners (Peter), Jacqueline Wells (Joan), Lucille Lund (Karen), Harry Cording (Thamal), Henry Armetta (Sergeant), Albert Conti (Lieutenant), Anna Duncan (Maid), Herman Bing (Car Steward), Andre Cheron (Conductor), Luis Alberni (Steward), George Davis (Bus Driver), Alphonse Martel (Porter), Tony Marlow (Brakeman), Albert Polet (Waiter), Peggy Terry, Lois January, Michael Mark, John George, Duskal Blane, King Baggott, John Peter Richmond [John Carradine], Harry Walker, Symona Boniface, Virginia Ains-worth, Paul Panzer (Cultists).

MARK OF THE VAMPIRE (1935 USA)

Released May 1, 1935; An MGM Production; *Director*: Tod Browning;

Screenplay: Guy Endore and Bernard Schubert (based on Browning's original story "The Hynotist"); *Additional Dialogue*: H.S. Kraft, Samuel Ornitz, and John L. Balderston; *Cinematographer*: James Wong Howe; *Art Director*: Cedric Gibbons; *Gowns*: Adrian; *Makeup*: Jack Dawn, William Tuttle; *Editor*: Ben Lewis; *Sound*: Douglas Shearer; 61 minutes; BBFC Certificate: A.

Lionel Barrymore (Prof. Zelen), Elizabeth Allen (Irena Borotyn), Bela Lugosi (Count Mora), Lionel Atwill (Insp. Neumann), Jean Hersholt (Baron Otto Von Zinden), Henry Wadsworth (Fedor), Donald Meek (Dr. Doskil), Jessie Ralph (Midwife), Ivan F. Simpson (Jan), Franklyn Ardell (Chauffeur), Leila Bennett (Maria), June Gittelson (Annie), Carroll Borland (Luna), Holmes Herbert (Sir Karel Borotyn), Michael S. Visaroff (Innkeeper), Rosemary Glosz (Innkeeper's Wife).

BRIDE OF FRANKENSTEIN (1935 USA)

Released May 6, 1935; A Universal Picture; *Director*: James Whale; *Producer*: Carl Laemmle, Jr.; *Screenplay*: William Hurlbut and John L. Balderston, based on Mary W. Shelley's characters; *Photography*: John Mescall; *Special Effects*: John P. Fulton; *Special Properties*: Kenneth Strickfaden; *Editor*: Ted Kent; *Art Director*: Charles D. Hall; *Music*: Franz Waxman; *Musical Director*: Mischa Bakaleinkoff; *Makeup*: Jack P. Pierce; *Sound*: Gilbert Kurland;

Assistant Directors: Harry Menke, Joseph McDonough; *Editorial Supervisor*: Maurice Pivar; 75 minutes; BBFC Certificate: A.

Boris Karloff (Monster), Colin Clive (Henry Frankenstein), Valerie Hobson (Elizabeth Frankenstein), Ernest Thesiger (Dr. Pretorius), Elsa Lanchester (Mary Shelley/"The Bride") Una O'Connor (Minnie), E.E. Clive (Burgomaster), O.P. Heggie (Hermit), Gavin Gordon (Lord Byron), Douglas Walton (Percy Shelley), Dwight Frye (Karl), Lucien Prival (Albert), Reginald Barlow (Hans), Mary Gordon (His Wife), Anne Darling (Shepherdess), Ted Billings (Ludwig), Neil Fitzgerald (Rudy), John Carradine, Robert Adair, John Curtis, Frank Terry (Hunters), Walter Brennan, Rollo Lloyd, Mary Stewart (Neighbors), Helen Parrish (Communion Girl), Arthur S. Byron (King), Joan Woodbury (Queen), Norman Ainsley (Archbishop), Peter Shaw (Devil), Kansas DeForrest (Ballerina), Josephine McKim (Mermaid), Billy Barty (baby).

WEREWOLF OF LONDON (1935 USA)

Released June 3, 1935; A Universal Picture; *Director*: Stuart Walker; *Producer*: Carl Laemmle; *Associate Producer*: Robert Harris; *Executive Producer*: Stanley Bergerman; *Screenplay*: John Colton, based on Robert Harris' story; Adapted by: Harvey Gates and Robert Harris; *Director of Photography*: Charles Stumar; *Special Photographic Effects*: John P. Fulton; *Assistant Directors*: Russell

Schoengarth and Milton Carruth; *Art Director*: Albert S. D'Agostino; *Music*: Karl Hajos; *Sound*: Gilbert Kurland; *Makeup*: Jack P. Pierce; 75 minutes; BBFC Certificate: A.

Henry Hull (Dr. Glendon), Warner Oland (Dr. Yogami), Valerie Hobson (Lisa Glendon), Lester Matthews (Paul), Spring Byington (Ettie Coombes), Lawrence Grant (Col. Forsythe), Clark Williams (Hugh Renwick), J.M. Kerrigan (Hawkins), Charlotte Granville (Lady Alice), Ethel Griffies (Mrs. Whack), Zeffie Tibbuvy (Mrs. Moncaster), Jeanne Bartlett (Daisy), Harry Stubbs (Jenkins), Louis Vincenot (Head Cooley), Reginald Barlow (Timothy), Eole Galil (The Prima Donna), Joseph North (Plimpton), Egon Brecher (Priest), Boyd Irwihn, Sr. (Hotel Manager), Helena Grant (Mother), Noel Kennedy (Boy), William Millman (John Buil), Tempe Pigott (Drunk Woman), Maude Leslie (Mrs. Charteris), Herbert Evans (Jenkins' Aide), David Thursby (Photographer), Gunnis Davis, George Kirby (Detectives), Jeffrey Hassel (Alf), Amber Norman (Beggar-Woman), James May (Bar-Man), Vera Buckland (Yogami's Housemaid), Wong Chung (Cooley), Roseollo Navello (Maid).

THE RAVEN (1935 USA)

Released July 22, 1935; A Universal Picture; *Director*: Louis Friedlander; *Producer*: David Diamond; *Screenplay*: David Boehm, suggested by Edgar Allan Poe's poem *The Raven* and short story *The Pit and the Pendulum*; *Director of Photography*: Charles Stumar; *Editor*: Albert Akst; *Supervising Editor*: Maurice Pivar; *Art Director*: Albert S. D'Agostino; *Sound Supervisor*: Gilbert Kurland; *Music Score*: Clifford Vaughan, Heinz Roemheld, and Y. Frank Harling; *Dance Sequence*: Theodore Kosloff; *Makeup*: Jack P. Pierce; *Assistant Directors*: Scott Beal, Victor Noerdlinger; *Dialogue Director*: Florence Enright; *Hairdresser*: Hazel Rogers; 61 minutes; BBFC Certificate: A.

Boris Karloff (Edmond Bateman), Bela Lugosi (Dr. Vollin), Lester Matthews (Dr. Halden), Irene Ware (Jean), Samuel S. Hinds (Judge Thatcher), Spencer Charters (Col. Grant), Inez Courtney (Mary), Ian Wolfe ("Pinky" Burns), Maidel Turner (Harnet Grant), Arthur Hoyt (Mr. Chapman), Jonathan Hale (Dr. Cook), Walter Miller (Dr. Hemingway), Cyril Thorton (Servant), Nina Golden (Dancer), Raine Bennett (Poe), Joe Haworth (Drug Clerk), Anne Darling, Mary Wallace, June Gittleson (Autograph Hunters), Bud Osborne (Policeman), Al Ferguson (Cook), Madeline Talcott (Nurse).

MAD LOVE (1935 USA)

Released August 2, 1935; An MGM Release; *Director*: Karl Freund; *Producer*: John W. Considine, Jr.; *Screenplay*: P.J. Wolfson and John L. Balderston; *Adaptation*: Guy Endore, from Maurice Renard's *Les Mains d'Orlac*; *Directors of Photography*: Chester Lyons and Gregg toland; *Music*: Dimitri Tiomkin; *Musical Director*: Oscar Radin; *Art Directors*: Cedric Gibbons, William A. Horning and Edwin B. Willis; *Wardrobe*: Dolly Tree; *Sound*: Douglas Shearer; *Editor*: Hugh Wynn; 68 minutes; UK title: *Hands of Orlac*; BBFC Certificate: A.

Peter Lorre (Dr. Gogol), Frances Drake (Yvonne Orlac), Colin Clive (Stephen Orlac), Ted Healy (Reagan), Sarah Haden (Marie), Isabel Jewell (Marianne), Edward Brophy (Rollo), Henry Kolker (Prefect), Harold Hubert (Thief), Keye Luke (Dr. Wong), Ian Wolfe (Henry Orlac), Charles Trowbridge (Dr. Marbeau), Murray Kinnell (Charles), May Beatty (Francoise), Rollo Lloyd (Endore), Nell Craig (Nurse Suzanne), Maurice Brierre (Taxi Driver), Julie Carter (Nurse), Christian Frank (Detective), Hooper Atchley (Conductor), Sam Ash, Robert Graves (Detectives), George Davis (Chauffeur), Otto Hoffman (Blind Man), Frank Darrien (Lavin), Robert Emmett Keane (Drunk), Ramsey Hill (Duke), Carl Stockdale (Notary), Al Borgato (Doorman), William Gibert (Frenchman), Harvey Clark (Station Master), Aphonz Ethier (Fingerprinter), Charles Hummel Wilson (Piano Man), Edward Lippy (Clerk), Roger Gray (Detective), Sarah Padden (Mother), Cora Sue Collins (Child), Russ Powsell (Gendarme), Earl M. Pingree (Detective), Jacques Vanier (Policeman), Mark Lubell (Prince), Matty Roubert (Newsboy), Edward Norris (Horror Show Patron), Rolfe Sedan (Gendarme), Michael Mark (Official).

THE INVISIBLE RAY (1936 USA)

Released January 20, 1936; A Universal Picture; *Director*: Lambert Hillyer; *Producer*: Edmund Grainger; *Screenplay*: John Colton, based on Howard Higgins and Douglas Hodges' story; *Director of Photography*: George Robinson; *Art Director*: Albert S. D'Agostino; *Special Photography*: John P. Fulton; *Music*: Franz Waxman; *Editor*: Bernard Burton; *Sound*: Gilbert Kurland; *Assistant Director*: Alfred Stern; *Technical Advisor*: Ted Behr; *Gowns*: Byrmer; 79 minutes; BBFC Certificate: A.

Boris Karloff (Dr. Janos Rukh), Bela Lugosi (Dr. Felix Benet), Frances Drake (Diana Rukh), Frank Lawton (Ronald Drake), Walter Kingsford (Sir Francis Stevens), Beulah Bondi (Lady Arabella Stevens), Violet Kemble Cooper (Mother Rukh), Nydia Westman (Briggs), Daniel Haines (Headman), Georges Ren-avent (Chief of the Surete), Paul Weigel (Monsieur Noyer), Adele St. Maur (Madame Noyer), Rank Rei-cher (Prof. Meiklejohn), Lawrence Stewart (Native "Boy"), Etta Mc-Daniel (Zulu Woman), Inex Seabury (Celeste), Winter Hall (Minster), Fred Toones (Snowflake), Hans Schumm (Attendant at Clinic), Lloyd Whitlock, Edward Davis, Edward Reinach (Scientists).

THE WALKING DEAD (1936 USA)

Released March 1936; A Warner Bros. Production; *Director*: Michael

Curtiz; *Producer*: Lou Edleman; *Screenplay*: Ewart Adamson, Peter Milne, Robert Andrews and Lillie Hayward, based on a story by Ewart Adamson and Joseph Fields; *Director of Photography*: Hal Mohr; *Editor*: Thomas Pratt; *Art Director*: Hugh Reticker; *Dialogue Director*: Irving Rappner; *Costumes*: Cary Odell; 65 minutes; BBFC Certificate: A.

Boris Karloff (John Ellman), Ricardo Cortez (Nolan), Edmund Gwenn (Dr. Beaumont), Marguerite Churchill (Nancy), Warren Hull (Jimmy), Barton MacLane (Loder), Henry O'Neill (Werner), Joseph King (Judge Shaw), Paul Harvey (Blackstone), Robert Strange (Merritt), Joseph Shaw (Trigger Smith), Eddie Acuff (Betcha), Ruth Robinson (Mrs. Shaw), Addison Richards (Prison Warden), Kenneth Harlan (Martin), Miki Morita (Sako), Adrian Rosley (Florist).

DRACULA'S DAUGHTER (1936 USA)

Released May 11, 1936; A Universal Picture; *Director*: Lambert Hillyer; *Associate Producer*: E.M. Asher; *Screenplay*: Garrett Fort, suggested by Oliver Jeffries; Based on Bram Stoker's *Dracula's Guest*; *Director of Photography*: George Robinson; *Art Director*: Albert S. D'Agostino; *Special Photography*: John P. Fulton; *Editor*: Milton Carruth; *Supervising Editor*: Maurice Pivar; *Music*: Edard Ward; *Sound*: Gilbert Kurland; *Makeup*: Jack P. Pierce; *Gowns*: Brymer; 70 minutes; BBFC Certificate: A.

Otto Kruger (Dr. Garth), Gloria Holden (Countess Marya Zaleska), Marguerite Churchill (Janet Blake), Edward Van Sloan (Dr. Von Helsing), Irving Pichel (Sandor), Nan Grey (Lili), Gilbert Emery (Sr. Basil Humphrey), Hedda Hooper (Lady Esme Hammond), E.E. Clive (Sgt. Wilkes), Billy Bevan (Albert), Halliwell Hobbes (Con. Hawkins), Claude Allister (Sir Aubrey Bedford), Edgar Norton (Hobbs), Eily Malyon (Miss Peabody).

THE DEVIL DOLL (1936 USA)

Released August 7, 1936; An MGM Production; *Director*: Tod Browning; *Executive Producer*: E.J. Mannix; *Screenplay*: Garrett Fort, Guy Endore and Erich von Stroheim; *Story*: Tod Browning, suggested by Abraham Merritt's novel *Burn! Witch! Burn!*; *Director of Photography*: Leonard Smith; *Art Director*: Cedric Gibbons; *Associate Art Directors*: Stan Rogers and Edwin B. Willis; *Editor*: Fredrick Y. Smith; *Music*: Franz Waxman; *Sound*: Douglas Shearer; *Wardrobe*: Dolly Tree; 70 minutes; BBFC Certificate; A.

Lionel Barrymore (Lavond), Maureen O'Sullivan (Lorraine), Frank Lawton (Toto), Rafaela Ottiano (Malita), Robert Greig (Coulvet), Lucy Beaumont (Mme. Lavond), Henry B. Walthall (Marcel), Grace Ford (Lachna), Pedro de Cordoba (Martin), Arthur Hohl (Rodin), Juanita Quigley (Marguerite), Claire du Brey (Mme. Coulvet), Rollo Lloyd (Detective), E. Allyn Warren (Commissioner).

THE MAN WHO CHANGED HIS MIND (1936 UK)

Released September 11, 1936; A Gaumont-British Production; *Director*: Robert Stevenson; *Producer*: Michael Balcon; *Associate Producers*: P. Edward Black and Sidney Gilliat; *Screenplay*: L. duGarde Peach, Sidney Gillat and John L. Balderston; *Director of Photography*: Jack Cox; *Art Director*: Alex Vetchinsky; *Editors*: R.E. Dearing and Alfred Roome; *Makeup*: Roy Ashton; *Music*: Louis Levy; *Sound*: W. Salter; Gowns: Molyneux; 65 minutes; BBFC Certificate: A; USA Title: *The Man Who Lived Again.*

Boris Karloff (Dr. Laurence), John Loder (Dick Haslewood), Anna Lee (Dr. Clare Wyatt), Frank Cellier (Lord Haslewood), Donald Calthrop (Clayton), Cecil Parker (Dr. Gratton), Lyn Harding (Prof. Holloway).

J'ACCUSE! (1937 France)

Released May 1937; A Forrester Parant Release; *Director*: Abel Gance; *Producer*: Gance; *Screenplay*: Gance; *Dialogue*: Steve Passeur; *Music*: Henry Verdun; *Camera*: Roger Hubert; BBFC Certificate H.

Victor Francen (Jean Diaz), Jean Max (Henri Chimay), Delaitre (François), Renée Devillers (Helene), Line Noro (Edith), Mary Lou (Flo).

THE THIRTEENTH CHAIR (1937 USA)

Released May 7, 1937; *Director*: George B. Seitz; *Screenplay*: Marion Parsonnet, based on Bayard Vellers' play; *Photography*: Charles Clarke; *Art Director*: Cedrick Gibbons; *Editor*: W. Don Hays; *Music*: David Snell; 68 minutes; BBFC Certificate: H.

Dame May Whitty (Mme. LaGrange), Madge Evans (Nell), Lewis Stone (Inspector Marney), Janet Beecher (Lady Crosby), Henry Daniell (Wales), Thomas Beck (Dick), Ralph Forbes (Lionel Trent), Holmes Herbert (Sir Roscoe), Heather Thatcher (Mary Eastwood), Charles Trowbridge (Dr. Mason), Robert Coote (Stanby), Elsa Buchanan (Miss Stanby).

SON OF FRANKENSTEIN (1939 USA)

Released January 13, 1939; A Universal Picture; *Director*: Rowland V. Lee; *Producer*: Rowland V. Lee; *Screenplay*: Willis Cooper; *Director of Photography*: George Robinson; *Art Director*: Jack Otterson; *Editor*: Ted Kent; *Music*: Charles Previn and Frank Skinner; *Sound*: Bernard B. Brown; *Set Decorator*: R. A. Gausman; *Gowns*: Vera West; *Assistant Director*: Fred Frank; 96 minutes; BBFC Certificate: H.

Basil Rathbone (Wolf Von Frankenstein), Boris Karloff (The Monster), Bela Lugosi (Ygor), Lionel Atwill (Inspector Krogh), Josephine Hutchinson (Elsa Von Frankenstein), Donnie Dunagan (Peter), Emma Dunn (Amelia), Edgar Norton (Benson), Perry Ivins (Fritz), Lawrence Grant (Burgomaster), Lionel Belmore (Lang), Michael Mark (Neumuller), Caroline Cook (Mrs.

Neumuller), Gustav Von Seyffertitz, Lorimer Johnson, Tom Ricketts (Burghers).

THE MAN THEY COULD NOT HANG (1939 USA)

Released August 17, 1939; A Columbia Picture; *Director*: Nick Grinde; *Producer*: Wallace MacDonald; *Screenplay*: Karl Brown; *Story*: Leslie T. White, George W. Sayre; *Director of Photography*: Benjamine Kline; *Editor*: William Lyon; *Music*: M. W. Stoloff; 65 minutes; BBFC Certificate: H.

Boris Karloff (Dr. Savaard), Lorna Gray (Janet Savaard), Robert Wilcox ("Scoop" Foley), Roger Pryor (Drake), Don Beddoe (Lt. Shane), Ann Dorian (Betty), Joseph DeStefani (Dr. Stoddard), Charles Trowbridge (Judge Bowman), Byron Foulger (Lang), James Craig (Watkins), John Tyrrell (Sutton).

THE DARK EYES OF LONDON (1939 UK)

Released November 1939; A Pathe Production; *Director*: Walter Summers; *Producer*: John Argyle; *Screenplay*: Patrick Kirwan and Walter Summers; *Novel*: Edgar Wallace; *Additional Dialogue*: Jan Van Lustil; *Director of Photography*: Bryan Langley; *Camera*: Ronald Anscombe; *Music*: Guy Jones; *Production Manager*: H.G. Inglis; *Sound*: A.E. Rudolph; *Editor*: E.G. Richards; *Art Director*: Duncan Sutherland; *Assistant Director*: Jack Martin; 75 minutes; BBFC Certificate: H; USA title: *The Human Monster*.

Bela Lugosi (Dr. Orloff), Hugh Williams (Inspector Holt), Greta Gynt (Diana Stewart), Edmond Ryan (Lt. O'Reilly), Wilfred Walter (Jake), Alexander Field (Grogan), Julie Suedo (Secretary), Arthur E. Owens (Dumb Lou), Gerald Pring (Henry Stewart), Charles Penrose (Drunk).

THE RETURN OF DR. X (1939 USA)

Released November 22, 1939; A Warner Bros./First National Production; *Director*: Vincent Sherman; *Producer*: Bryan Foy; *Screenplay*: Lee Katz; *Original Story*: William J. Makin's *The Doctor's Secret*; *Director of Photography*: Sid Hickox; *Editor*: Thomas Pratt; *Art Director*: Esdras Hartley; *Sound*: Charles Lang; *Gowns*: Milo Anderson; *Technical Advisor*: Dr. Leo Schulman; *Makeup*: Pere Westmore; 62 minutes; BBFC Certificate: H.

Wayne Morris (Walter Garrett), Rosemary Lane (Joan Vance), Humphrey Bogart (Quesne), Dennis Morgan (Michael Rhodes), John Litel (Dr. Flegg), Lya Lys (Angela Merrova), Huntz Hall (Pinky), Charles Wilson (Det. Kincaid), Vera Lewis (Miss Sweetman), Howard Hickman (Chairman), Olin Howland (Undertaker).

Bibliography

Books

Brunas, Michael, John Brunas and Tom Weaver. *Universal Horrors*. Jefferson, NC: McFarland, 1990.
Katz, Ephraim. *The Film Encyclopedia*. New York: Crowell, 1979.
Lenning, Arthur. *The Count*. New York: Putnam, 1974.
Mank, Gregory W. *It's Alive!* LaJulla, CA: Barnes, 1981.
____. *Karloff and Lugosi*. Jefferson, NC: McFarland, 1990.
____. *Hollywood Cauldron*. Jefferson, NC: McFarland, 1994.
Mathews, Tom Dewe. *Censored*. London: Chatto & Windus, 1994.
Senn, Bryan. *Golden Horrors*. Jefferson, NC: McFarland, 1996.
Skal, David J. *The Monster Show*. New York: Norton, 1993.
Skal, David J., and Elias Savada. *Dark Carnival*. New York: Anchor, 1995.

Periodicals

Cult Movies, Editor Buddy Barnett, North Hollywood, CA.
The Kinematograph Weekly, London.
Today's Cinema, London.

Index

Numbers in **boldface** refer to pages with photographs.

Index